Commentaries on Hebrew and Christian Mythology

By Parish B. Ladd

Judge of the San Francisco Bar

Published by Pantianos Classics

ISBN-13: 978-1-78987-546-1

First published in 1896

Contents

Preface

The claim which has so long been persistently maintained of the supernatural origin of Christianity and its Christ has at last been met by positive denials, and thereby an issue has been raised.

Because of the natural difficulty of proving a negative, the rule has long since been permanently established that he who asserts a thing which is denied must first offer proofs sufficient to make a prima-facie case, before the party denying the allegation is called upon for a defense.

Has the church ever made sufficient proof that its religion and its founder were of supernatural origin to call for counter-evidence? We think not; but this claim has been made, and for nearly nineteen hundred years it has been acquiesced in by a very large and respectable body of men calling themselves Christians.

It may be said, not without some show of reason, that this long acquiescence is equivalent to proof sufficient to make a prima-facie case.

Assuming such to be true, we are put on the defensive, but with the right to enter a special plea as to the force of the proof offered by the church, and under this plea we may criticise the church's position, and inquire: First, whether such a man as Christ is said to have been ever lived; second, if he be a real person, then what do we know of and concerning his sayings and doings.

There never has been a time when public sentiment so emphatically demanded a clearer insight into the groundwork or origin of Christianity as at this time.

This is an age of unrest, an age of intelligence: the masses of our people are thinking for themselves; they are no longer satisfied to accept the dogmatic expressions of the priest and clergyman on these issues; they are determined to investigate, to look into the foundation of a system of religion which seems to them to violate the well-recognized rules of natural law, and thereby conflict with their common sense.

They are told by their priests and clergymen that their Christ was the son of the creator of the universe, begotten of an earthly woman, and that their creed, or system of religion, is also of divine origin.

Notwithstanding the long acquiescence in this claim, the default has been set aside, and the case put on the calendar for a trial on its merits.

The question here presents itself: How is the proof to be obtained, and where is it to be found? The great mass of our people have been and are too much engrossed in business to have kept up with the numerous works of critics, scientists, and historians which have been published in the last fifty years, or to even suspect where the needed evidence lies. Very few, even intelligent people, know anything concerning ancient history, as studied from the ruins of monuments of Chaldea, Egypt, and Assyria, or the numerous works of science and criticism which have so shaken old opinions and beliefs.

The facts disclosed by these works are practically out of the reach of most people, because they have not the time or patience to hunt up and wade through hundreds of volumes to obtain such knowledge.

The aim of the author of this little work, after years of toil among the voluminous works on different branches of this subject, has been to collect, collate, arrange, and condense from the writings of others, the matters bearing directly on the several points under discussion herein; to state the facts and conclusions in a clear and concise manner, so as to afford to most readers all of the desired information as to the origin or foundation of Christianity and its Christ; also the foundation of Judaism, on which Christianity rests.

The evidence so collected, and presented herein, we think, clearly establishes the following facts, to wit: That Judaism rests on myths borrowed and copied from legends in common use among all of the Oriental nations; that Abraham was a myth; that Moses has been buried beneath the debris of legends which from time to time enveloped him; that the Pentateuch, the so-called five books of Moses, was not written by Moses, nor until from five hundred to a thousand years after his death; that the Bible story of the creation, of Adam and Eve, as well as the flood, are but myths borrowed from legends and copied into Hebrew scriptures.

As to Christianity and its founder, we think the evidence raises a serious doubt of the man's existence; that if he ever did live, the fathers of the church have never been able to find out when he was born or when he died, or to fix the real time within more than one hundred years; that the time given in the scriptures was arbitrarily fixed by the church in furtherance of its interests and at the expense of truth; that of the sayings and doings of Christ little or nothing is definitely known; that the four Gospels and other Christian writings are forgeries, and were made up from tradition, letters, and scraps picked up here and there, voted into the Canon in the interest of the church, to which have been added, at different times, such matters and things as suited the church; that much of the sacred writings was the result of force, fraud, and bribery.

In point of morality, after citing and comparing most of the pagan religions with Christianity, we find them all superior to the latter.

As to the leaders of the church, Catholic and Protestant, the evidence shows them to have been dogmatic, superstitious, intolerant, and cruel in the extreme; that to perpetuate their power and rule, they have put to death more than 30,000,000 of innocent men, women, and children, a very large proportion of whom were tortured in a manner only conceivable by fiends.

Commentaries on Hebrew and Christian Mythology

Primitive Divinities — How Made

In the Hebrew Genesis we are told that Abraham came out of Ur of the Chaldees. The city of Ur at the time of the mythical Abraham, was the capital of Elam. At the dawn of history, some four thousand years B. C, the whole country from the Persian Gulf to the Zagras Mountains was known as Mesopotamia. The low flat country of the south, bordering on the Persian Gulf, was known as Accadia. Accadia, at that early date, was divided into small districts; each district had a capital city in which a large temple was erected for the worship of the divinities. Each capital was governed by a Pator, being king and priest in one, and each city had its special deity. Prior thereto, at that time, and for a long time thereafter, not only in Asia but in most parts of Europe, each household had its divine protector and its sacred fire, in which household, at first the father, and in later times the Pator, or priest, resided and ruled the family. This is believed to be the origin of the great family of Gods, who since that time have presided over the inhabitants of the earth.

After the organization of the tribes, and building of cities, it became necessary to appoint or establish municipal deities with enlarged powers to preside over the tribe and city as the household Gods had presided over the family.

Notwithstanding this tribal or city God, it was a long time before the household divinity became obsolete, for we are told in Hebrew mythology that even Abraham had his household Gods at the city of Ur. These family divinities in later times became known as Talismans.

When a tribal or municipal deity was created, he was named by the joint action of all the Pators, or forced on the people by the ruling faction, and his powers and duties were by this body defined and established.

When several tribes or cities had united, as they did for mutual protection, into kingdoms or empires, Gods for such kingdoms and empires were created by the joint action of all the Pators, or their representatives, of such kingdoms and empires, sanctioned by the sovereign, who generally sat in and presided over the council. The last council of this character held its session at Nice, and was presided over by the great Constantine. No one of these Gods ever arose to the dignity of presiding over the world until after the reign of Solomon, when the kingdoms of Judah and Israel cast off Ab-Ram and Elohim, and out of the debris created Jehovah.

Divinities Selected in the Heavens

In the creation or selection of deities, the material was sought for in the heavens. The Sun was everywhere selected as the head or national divinity;

9

out of the other planets and from natural phenomena other and lesser Gods were made. The Sun being the source of light, heat, and life, there could be nothing more natural than that it should be selected to occupy the first and highest place in the heavens and in the affections of man. The head of these celestial divinities was given, or supposed to possess, unlimited wisdom, and power over all lesser Gods, and over man. Early man, realizing pleasure and pain, the former good and the latter bad, naturally deduced therefrom a dual principle; so he created an evil being, and fixed his abode in and below the earth. Having thereby created good and evil beings, representing good and evil principles, he naturally concluded that these good and evil beings must be at war with each other; and as he had created these two beings with no higher type than his own to model from, he created them in his own image; to the one he gave his good attributes, and to the other ascribed his evil, dark nature. Now, as man loved light, and the numerous blessings it brought to him, he looked up, welcomed the dawn, worshiped the sun in its onward course through the heavens, and went to his cave or cabin in mortal dread and fear of wild beasts and other evils, where he poured out his prayers for the return of the solar orb.

Such was man in his savage and semi-savage state, in his nomadic life. He had thus created for himself a system of celestial beings, on whom he could call for help in time of need; he had made them in his own image because he had no higher type to work from.

These divine beings have ever been created by man in his savage and semi-savage state; they were the natural products of his own ignorance of the laws of nature. The various phenomena of nature, he being unable to account for them, were ascribed to this mysterious power. Having created these beings and worshiped them in his savage and semi-savage state, he left them as an inheritance for later generations. While civilized man could tolerate and worship these stale, antiquated Gods, because of long standing, he could never tolerate the creation of new ones. It remained for the Council of Nice to create the last of these heavenly rulers. Having created the Gods out of the heavenly bodies and the phenomena of nature, and believing that they were, like himself, endowed with will power, and could do him good and harm, he naturally sought to propitiate them, to get their good will and to secure their aid. To do this, he offered prayers, sacrifices, and entreaties invoking special powers. Nor is it strange that, in the course of time, he should come to believe that he received such powers. The Accadian mythology (says the Encyclopaedia Britannica) had its origin in astrology; the stars were personified and became Gods. The Semites accepted this system, which was handed down to the Jews, and later was adopted by the Christians, and the devil, with horns, claws, tail, and wings, as found on the Assyrian bas-reliefs, was copied by the Christians.

Origin of the Priesthood

During all this time there grew up a class of men more cunning, if not more wise, than the populace, who pretended and claimed to see and converse with the Gods, face to face, and to be able to obtain special favors for those not versed in hidden mysteries.

It being to the interest of these mediators to encourage the belief in their special powers, and finding the uninitiated ready believers, the priests soon gained influence, control, and even dominion over their unsuspecting subjects, who became blind devotees of their wily priests.

In order to retain their influence, power, and dominion, these crafty pretenders promulgated laws, rules, and precepts for the observance, guidance, and control of their dupes and votaries.

That these laws, rules, and precepts came directly from the Gods has ever been the pretense of the priests in every religious system; and as such they have been too sacred to be questioned, at least by the uninitiated multitude, and so the great unthinking mass of mankind have at all times accepted, without thought, question, or murmur, the Gods and laws so made, as divine truths.

In this way a priesthood under different names was very early established, and became a fixture and a power among all, or nearly all, of the peoples and tribes of the earth. This power and dominion did little harm to man in his barbaric or semi-civilized state, nor was its baneful influence materially felt until a later day, when this ecclesiastical power was extended over the civilian as a citizen or subject of the state, and the people found themselves within the grasp of this divine octopus.

The people so priest-ridden found it easier or more agreeable to accept without question what was given them by a class of men whom they looked upon as possessed of great wisdom and divine power than to think for themselves. These beliefs, so accepted and acted upon, having been handed down from generation to generation, and from century to century, became part and parcel of man's very nature; nor has it been an easy matter for more enlightened men to throw off this long-established network of myths, fables, and falsehoods. Some men nominally accept these beliefs because it is to their interest to do so; others because it is less trouble to follow an established error than to oppose it.

The true believer of to-day, if there be any such, finds himself compelled in religious matters to lay aside his reason and even his common sense; his religion is constantly at war with natural law; though he may for a time succeed in driving out nature, she is sure to return to claim her own. Time obliterates his false religion when nature calls him back home again, for nature is never at variance with sound reason and philosophy.

These priests in early times made images or statues of their Gods, and set them up in dense forests and other lonely places, where they spent most of their time in prayers and solemn festivals, and where they acted as inter-

11

preters of the divine will for and at the call of the devotee. These images were sometimes attached to hidden springs and machines, which were worked to produce sounds in the presence of the dupes, and these noises were interpreted by the priest as best suited his purpose. In Egypt, as late as the time of Moses, the Egyptian and Hebrew priests adopted a system of chance, the result of which was interpreted for good or evil as best suited the caller and best worked in the interest of the priest. In later times, the Hebrew substituted for the oracle, the dreamer and the prophet. On this subject, Ernest Renan, one of the greatest of biblical scholars and critics, in his "History of Israel" says: "Man created a divine world in his own image, and treated the Gods of it as he liked to be treated by his inferiors. There was an exchange of politeness between trembling man and the potent forces by which he believed himself to be surrounded. Primitive man saw in thunder naught else but the explosion of the wrath of an all-powerful being dwelling in the clouds and on the summits of mountains. This primitive man, in his savage simplicity, his senses scarcely at all developed, became the dupe of his own hallucinations."

This author further says: "It has never been discovered that a supreme being concerns himself with events either of a physical or moral order; no signs have been discovered in nature of any intelligent agent superior to man; nature is inexorable, its laws are blind; prayer never encounters any being that it can turn from its purpose."

As to the effect of prayer, this author only states what every man of common sense knows to be true. But, it may be asked, Why is prayer kept up? The answer is obvious: Clergymen get their living by it; and as to others, some are too ignorant to understand anything, and some act from force of habit.

The philosophers of Greece and Rome, ever refusing to accept the religion of their times, were by the pious denounced as Infidels and Atheists. These religious men claimed that what had been believed and maintained by pious men in olden times, and had stood the test of ages, must be true, but, says Renan, "Philosophy and reason dispelled ignorance, created doubts, and finally religion was buried beneath its myths and fables."

Robert Burton, the author of "The Anatomy of Melancholy," made an apt statement when he said, "Ignorance is the mother of devotion." The proof of this is shown by the facts that the three most religious nations in the world, Spain, Italy, and Portugal, exhibit an average of seventy-three persons out of* every hundred who can neither read nor write, while Germany, France, England, and the United States average less than eight per cent, who cannot read or write. Germany, the least religious of all, has less than one-half of one per cent, who cannot read or write, while in Mexico, and the Central and South American states, nearly all of the educated people are Freethinkers, and nearly all, if not all, of the ignorant belong to the church.

Chaldea, its Territory, People, Religion, and Language

First: Its Territory. — Before proceeding to the discussion of Hebrew mythology, it will be in order, first, to take a cursory view of Chaldea, its territory, people, religion, and language, which have contributed so largely to the stock of ideas held and promulgated by the tribes of Israel.

The Hebrews were of Semitic stock or origin, and are supposed to have led a primitive life in Arabia, whence they migrated to Chaldea, some of them settling in the city of Ur. At a very early date, and before Chaldea had risen to a state of importance, the eastern part of the country was known as Elam, of which Ur was the capital city; and when the territory of Elam had ceased to exist as a separate kingdom, and had been lost or merged in Chaldea, Ur remained for a time the principal city of the Chaldees. It was located on the west branch of the Euphrates, near where that river, at that early time, entered the Persian Gulf. The territory of Elam never extended north of the low flat country at the head of that gulf, but it extended east over the land of Persia. Dungi, one of its earliest known kings, ruled over the country at least as early as 2400 years B. C. About 2200 years B. C. the Elamites overran and conquered the land of Chaldea, which lay at the north of Elam; and about 2000 B. C. Chaldea united with Babylon, and under their king, Chedorlaomar, war was made on Elam, which, after a long struggle, surrendered. These peoples, being merged into one, fixed their capital at Ur. From this time on, the country remained under one monarch under the general appellation of Chaldea or Chaldeo-Babylonia, under which name or names it continued to grow in wealth and power for a long period. The capital being finally removed to the city of Babylon, the country took the name of Babylonia.

According to the opinion of most historians, the mythical Abraham became a prominent figure in the city of Ur of the Chaldees, about 2000 B. C, but according to the reckoning of Josephus, Abraham lived about 1836 B. C.

About 2000 B. C. the country was invaded from Arabia by a people known as Semites. This people set up their rulers and held the country for a short period, when Babylon threw off this foreign yoke, and re-established her power; but the wars which followed between Babylon and Assyria put the former in a position to pay tribute to the latter for short periods. Finally Babylon fell a prey to its more powerful neighbor on the north, and became a part of the Assyrian Empire.

When Assyria fell under the yoke of Persia, Babylon ceased to exist, but the great city retained its name and influence until its final destruction by Alexander the Great, 332 B.C.

The People of Chaldea

Second: The People of Chaldea. — It is said, and often repeated by historians, with some discrepancy of opinion, that the whole of the country called

Mesopotamia was settled by a yellow race called Turanian; and that the Aryans or white race migrated from southern Russia or Afghanistan, and mixed with the Turanian, thereby creating a new stock. It is also both asserted and denied that Ethiopia sent into this country some of her people called Cushites, who had. curly or woolly hair, who, with the Semites from Arabia, made up the Chaldea-Babylonian race.

Let it be here said that, while very much has been asserted by historians as to the prehistoric migrations of the various races of mankind, very little is known; most of such statements are mere conjecture. Every country at the dawn of history has been found peopled by a race who asserted that they had come into the country from elsewhere, and had either driven out, exterminated, or mixed with the people found there. It is quite well established that the Chaldeans differed but slightly in appearance, manners, customs, and religion from the numerous tribes or peoples who at that epoch lived in the country bordering on the eastern shores of the Mediterranean, and more especially the Canaanites.

Now let us return and see how near we can fix the date when the little band of Semites conceived the first idea of the oneness of divine power, and from what source they derived it. As to the time when the so-called Abraham of the Chaldees resided at Ur, authors do not agree. Josephus says that the 430 years which is the biblical account of the time the Hebrews were in Egypt, were evenly divided between Palestine and Egypt, 215 years in each country. If this be correct, assuming that Moses lived 1400 B. C., it would fix Abraham's time in Chaldea at 1800 B. C.; but this does not agree with the account given by numerous other historians. While all agree that Josephus was an honest historian, the same opinion says that he was very inaccurate. It is quite certain that he did not have the resources for his facts that we possess concerning Abraham and Moses. As to the time of Moses, authorities differ, placing him from 1300 to 1500 B. C. Several fix the time at 1315 to 1320 B.C., and this seems the more reliable. Assuming the time of Moses to be 1320 B.C., we shall find Abraham at Ur about 2100 B.C. It becomes important to know what were the religious sentiments of the people of Ur of the Chaldees at this date, so as to find the source from which sprang the notion of a single divinity. We have ample evidence that the Chaldean divinities were numerous at that time. They were divided into three classes. The third class was extremely numerous, comprising many of the household Gods which had not become extinct. The first two classes were made up of trinities. The names of the three comprising the first class were Anu, El, and Hea; El is often called Bell, and Hea called Ea.

We will now proceed to speak of the first triad, who, as it will hereafter appear, were the progenitors of Jehovah. Of these celestial beings, Anu, El, and Hea, each possessed special attributes and was assigned special duties. In that age of the world the tendency was to personify the heavenly bodies, the phenomena of nature, the rivers, mountains, peoples, tribes, and nations;

14

in short, nearly every important thing and event received an individual name. These three divinities were the personified representatives of the sun, the earth, and the waters.

Anu had his abode in the upper heavens beyond the reach of mortal eyes, and so was little known and worshiped; he had a general supervision over the lesser Gods, and a temple at Erech. El was the creator of all things, the manager and general superintendent over all mankind; he created the heavens and the earth, divided the land from the waters, and, according to the Chaldean legends, which have come down to us in writing, he made man out of the dust of the earth, and called him Admi. He also created the beasts of the field, the fowls of the air, and the fishes and monsters of the deep. He gave Admi a wife, and placed the pair in a garden through which flowed four rivers. The pair were commanded by El not to eat of the fruit of a certain tree; they were tempted by a serpent, disobeyed the command, and were for this reason driven from the garden and a flaming sword was put at the gate to prevent a re-entry. This legend was a representation of nature. Admi and the woman were but personifications of earth and water; all of which we will describe more fully hereafter when we come to compare the biblical account of this matter with the Chaldean account of it, as given in the inscriptions taken out of the ruins of the cities in that country.

El was also a God of war, had his temples in all the cities of Chaldea, and was worshiped from the Indus to the Nile. The sun became the emblem of El, and as the animal and vegetable kingdoms were produced and supported by the light and heat of that orb, so El became the first object of worship. It was to him that prayers and sacrifices were offered; he was the giver of the harvest, and of all things which administered to the comfort and happiness of man. In the course of time Anu and Hea were regarded as separate attributes of the all-powerful Elo, representing the three cardinal virtues of life; knowledge, goodness, and power.

Standing by themselves, they were three Gods personified as Anu, El, and Hea, but when merged into one, the one took the name of Elohim. It will be remembered that the Hebrews used indiscriminately the names of El and Elohim down to the time of the exodus from Egypt, and to some extent these names were in use by them in connection with Iahveh until the time of David and Solomon, when Iahveh or Jehovah was substituted. It is now generally believed that the true pronunciation is Jahwe, or Yahwe, says the Encyclopaedia Britannica.

Hea, when standing alone, was the God of the nether world, the waters of Hades and the spirits of darkness. Of the second-class divinities stood Merodah, Arabel, and Sharmis. The first had a shrine at Babylon, the second resided at Muru, while the third ruled at Larsa and Sippara. The Goddess Ishtar, daughter of Hea, was the most beloved of all the divinities; she had her temples in all of the principal cities. Such was the religious sentiment in the land of the Euphrates, at the time of Abraham.

15

Abraham, Was He a Myth?

Now let us go back and take a look at Abraham in the city of Ur of the Chaldees, where the Hebrew legends find him a genuine person; and if he be such, we will go with him out of that land, cross the Euphrates, stop at Haran, the city of the moon God, for two or more years, and then travel with him into the promised land.

The word Abraham was written and pronounced at Elan, "Orham, Aborham, and Ab-Ram." Some archaeologists have asserted and maintained, not without a fair degree of evidence, that the word Abraham applied to a tribe. This name appears on the inscriptions found among the ruins of that country as Aborham, who was one of the Gods. At least one of the tribes which migrated from Ur to Canaan was designated as Ab-Ram.

Renan, the great archaeologist and biblical critic, says: "The inhabitants of Padan Aram were particularly attached to the legend of the fabled Orham, king of Ur, and called him Aborham; who was represented sometimes as a man, and at other times as a God. The tribes originally ascribed to him the part of supreme ancestor and divine patriarch; the Hebrews pronounced his name Abraham, which they interpreted, father of many nations, but they often called him Ab-Ram, the mighty father."

Renan also informs us that the Ishmaelites, the Midianites, and the whole series of Arab tribes grouped under the names of Cuthura and Agar, were classed as Abramites; that their manners, customs, and language were much the same; and that they formed one vast brotherhood from Haran to southern Palestine. This author further says that among the tribes devoted to the worship of El, connected with the mythical Abraham, was Israel; that Beni Jacob, or Beni Israel, was the name of a tribe which, in the course of time, became personified under the name of Jacob, and that this tribe worshiped El; that Lot, like Abraham, was but the personification of another tribe. Philo, an Alexandrian Jew, of the priestly order, born twenty to ten years B.C., taught and wrote that Abraham, Isaac, and Jacob were but personifications of three phases or elements of virtue; and such were the teachings of the Rabbinical schools of Palestine, long after the return of the Hebrews from Egypt. This school also taught that the Pentateuch and the legends of Moses were but allegorical; its literal interpretation was an absurdity, says Philo. In order to make Judaism palatable to the refined Greeks, Philo attempted to prove to them that it was the same as their philosophy.

Having disposed of Abraham as a myth, let us return and follow the growth of Israel, from the little germ formed at Ur, until it has become a power in the land.

About 2200 years B. C. the plurality of divinities in Chaldea had reached its limit, when, at least, the Semites were ripe for a change.

The Germ of Judaism formed at Ur of the Chaldees

It has been maintained with much force by eminent scholars, that man never originates within himself an idea; that all new conceptions are suggested to him by some object in nature, which he grasps and molds into form.

Taking such historical facts as we find before us, and proceeding according to the method of induction, may we not safely say that a little group of Semites had banded themselves together to remold or adjust the prevailing system of divinities? The city of Ur was in a hot country; this little band assembled at noonday under the wide-spreading branches of the fig tree. There they talked over the traditions concerning the powers of heaven, in which they saw Gods contending in battle among themselves, in like manner as the tribes of the earth. They also repeated the legends of creation, of Adam and Eve, of a great flood, and many other marvelous occurrences; and they wondered if all these things were true. They read in this tradition that in bygone times Asia was divided up into small tribes, constantly at war with each other; they saw their own country ruled over by a king, a single monarch, who governed and protected his people and gave them peace and happiness, and if a single monarch on earth (for Asia was the earth to them), why not a single monarch in the heavens? They had thus borrowed the germ, and grasped at its utility.

From this little beginning sprang the ten tribes of Israel, who created the Rabbi, who established the ephod, which was replaced by the oracles, which made the prophets who foretold the Messiah, who selected the apostles, who laid the egg that hatched the priestlet, who established the Inquisition that drove the stake and kindled the fire that consumed unbelievers.

Let us now see what this little body of Semites did at Ur. Anu was a God without a record and almost without a following; Hea was the God of the nether world; while El, our great solar orb, was the creator of all things. Why retain the other two? Of what use were they? And as for the other classes of divinities, they were countless. Why not accept and adore El as the sole God, even if we have to accept his consolidated name, Elohim? And so this little band conceived and promulgated the theory of a single God; and as they had made him, why should he not become the God of this people — a special divinity, a tribal El? And as he became their God, so they became his children, the children of El. In the language of that country, to say that they were his children, was to say Isra-El.

But there was another faction at Ur, which was at a later date called the children of Ab-Ram; although their early history is in doubt. If Ab-Ram, afterward called Abraham, was one of the mythological demigods of Elam who ruled the country for millions of years, then the matter explains itself by showing that the other faction, though monotheists like the Israelites, simply chose another divinity in the place of El.

17

If we can give any credence to Hebrew legends, the Abramites left Ur of the Chaldees for the land of Canaan about seven hundred years before Moses, or four hundred and thirty years, according to Josephus. Whether they were driven out in consequence of their opinions and teachings of monotheism, or whether they left of their own volition, must ever remain in doubt, for history is silent on this point. If we allow ourselves to speculate on probabilities, we may assume that their departure was voluntary, for although they were monotheists, they were not entirely weaned from the worship of the numerous Gods of the country, for they often relapsed into their old practices and offered up prayers to Anu, El, and Hea, and even to their household divinities.

Semites Cross the Euphrates and Become Hebrews

Prior to the time of their migration to the west, these people were classed under the general head of Semites, but when they left their native country and crossed the Euphrates, they became emigrants. The term emigrant, in the language of that country, especially when applied to those who had crossed waters, was expressed by the word Hebrew. The word Hebrew, in their dialect, is the equivalent of emigrant in English; in other words, they are convertible terms. This people from that time, and in consequence of that act, became Hebrews.

The biblical legends, treating Abraham as a man, make him stop at Haran for over two years. Haran was a large city, and the home of Sin, the moon God, who had a great temple there. The moon deity was a favorite in Chaldea, owing to the fact that the sun's heat in that dry, parched-up country made it necessary for most of the travel and much of the work to be performed at night, when the moon afforded light without heat.

What object could have induced the Abramites to tarry so long at Haran, the Mecca of the moon God, other than the worship of that divinity? That they did worship at that shrine we have ample evidence. After this long stay at Haran, the Abramites moved on to Canaan.

The history of the Israelites from this time until their return from Egypt is very meager; in short, what is claimed as knowledge on this subject is little better than guess. Some few things, however, are quite well established, among which it may be said that they were a nomadic people, herding their flocks, and living on the milk and flesh of their animals. What little knowledge they possessed was confined to the priestly order.

If we accept the biblical account of 430 years in Egypt, and 600 years in all, then this people remained in Canaan 170 years. If we accept Josephus' account, the time spent in Palestine was 215 years.

From the foregoing we have learned that Ab-Ram, afterward called, by the Hebrews, Abraham, was at an early date treated as one of the Gods of Elam, and we are also in possession of other facts tending to show that Abraham was the tribal God of the Abramites, afterward known as Judaites, or the tribe of Judah. We have ample evidence that there were at Elam several peoples, or tribes, known as Semites, and that the tendency of all the Semitic peoples was toward monotheism, and that the tribe or clan which afterward became known as Israelites, not only while in Elam and Chaldea, but for a long time thereafter and until the end of the reign of Solomon, continued to worship the Chaldean God, El. History also informs us that about 2,000 B. C. the Abramites migrated from Ur of the Chaldees to the land of Canaan, but when the Israelites left Elam the records are silent. We first learn of that people in Canaan, where the Abramites and the Israelites lived entirely separate, with nothing in common, other than that both were monotheists.

We also learn that the two peoples went into Egypt at different times, each going by itself, and that they did not fraternize in the land of the Pharaohs; we also learn that the Abramites, or at least their priests, on leaving Egypt cast off the God Ab-Ram and accepted the Egyptian Iahveh. After their return to Canaan their history becomes quite clear. The Israelites, worshipers of El, or Elohim, settled in the north, and the Abramites, former worshipers of Ab-Ram, now, at least so far as their priests were concerned, worshipers of Iahveh, settled at the south, with Jerusalem as their capital.

Mr. Renan et al inform us that during the reigns of David and Solomon, each tribe, or people, commenced to write up, from tradition, the stories of creation, of the flood and the history of Moses, and that the two peoples, or their priests, continued each to worship its own God until about the close of the reign of Solomon, when both agreed on Iahveh or Jehovah, as the one divinity in the place and stead of Elohim and Ab-Ram. But the names, Jew for the tribe of Judah, and Israel for the worshipers of El, or Elohim, still remain distinct, being used indiscriminately for both peoples.

The Hebrews Go into Egypt

Renan says: "The first emigration of the Hebrews into Egypt was composed of the Beni-Israel; which took place at two different times. The first division seems to have been on good terms with the Hittites of Egypt, while the bulk of the tribe remained on the best of terms with the Hittites of Hebron. The first division, which settled in Egypt, was called the clan of Josephel, or the Beni-Joseph. The second lot, finding the Josephel Hebrews well settled, followed and settled in the land of Goshen, but the different factions did not fraternize."

This author informs us that the Hebrews at this time had no writings, and that it appears, from the most trustworthy authority we have, that their sojourn in Egypt was only about one hundred years. As to the exodus, he concludes that it took place under Seti II; but we cannot accept these statements as true in the face of other evidence. The time spent in Canaan could not, according to some authorities, have exceeded one hundred years. Renan, one of our best authorities, fixes the time at one hundred years. This is probably

19

predicated largely on natural increase and the small number of people who, at the date of the exodus, could have found support on the desert of Paran, even for as short a period as two years; but it will be seen that these statements do not support either the biblical account or Josephus; for, according to the former, we have 700 years; and by the latter, we have 430 years.

On this state of the evidence, we shall be forced to conclude that no definite time can be fixed in either place.

Egyptian Influence on the Hebrew

That the Hebrews while in Egypt adopted the religion and other practices of the Egyptians, seems to admit of no doubt. They worshiped Astata and Iahveh, also Adoni, the sun God; they also joined the Egyptians in the worship of other local divinities; but in these practices they did not forget Elohim, the sun God of Chaldea. They also adopted most of the religious ceremonies and customs of the people with whom they were located, as will be shown further on. These numerous divinities continued to be worshiped by the Hebrews up to the time of Moses, when the priests attempted to substitute Iahveh in conjunction with Elohim in the place and stead of all other deities, for they were not unmindful of the fact that their people, while in Egypt, had lost sight of the one-god theory in the worship of the numerous divinities of the Egyptians. As the great body of the Hebrews were extremely ignorant, it was no easy task of the priests to turn them from their newly-acquired idols, and this is fully illustrated by the fact that even Aaron, while at Sinai, set up the golden calf, the Apis bull of Egypt, and the brazen serpent for his people to worship. Even up to the time of Rehoboam, the Egyptian with many of the Canaanite divinities were not only favorites of the people, but even of some of the priests of Israel.

Hebrews as Herdsmen in Egypt

The migration of the Hebrews from Canaan into Egypt was owing to the drouth, and the failure to obtain feed for their cattle in Canaan, for the Jews were living in tents and moving from place to place with their herds in search of better pasture; they had obtained permission from the Egyptians to live and pasture their herds on the lowlands of the delta near the Mediterranean. They went there in two bodies at different times, Josephus says "seventy souls in all, and after two hundred and fifteen years they left the country with 800,000 men, besides women and children." If to this last number we add women and children, the whole number at the time of their exit out of Egypt, could not have been less than 3,000,000. This statement must be erroneous, for nearly all the Hebrews .of Canaan went into Egypt, and as they had resided in the former country for at least one or two hundred years. their number must have far exceeded seventy souls; probably they num-

20

bered several thousands. And as to the statement that their number at the exodus was 800,000 men, this must have been overdrawn, for, as they depended on the scanty products of the desert for subsistence, it is hardly to be credited that such a large army could have found sufficient food during the long stay in the desert.

Hebrews as Nomads

Let it be remembered that the Hebrews, during all the period of time while in Chaldea, in Canaan, in Egypt, and long after their return to the promised land, remained a nomadic people, having no fixed abode, living in tents and on the milk and flesh of their animals, wandering from place to place, and from pasture to pasture, in search of feed for their stock. Rich in herds and in ignorance, the Hebrews thus lived in blissful simplicity, dreaming of a celestial paradise ruled over by a single God, our solar orb, under the consolidated name of Elohim, until exchanged by Moses for Jehovah. Thus they continued to live for more than a thousand years after all the peoples and nations around them had reached a high state of civilization.

Geology and history teach us that man passes through three stages of existence. First, he is a savage, a hunter, living on game and wild fruits. Second, from the savage state he passes into a barbarous or semi-civilized state, living on the milk and flesh of his herds, and wandering from place to place. Lastly, he emerges from his semi-savage, nomadic condition, becomes a tiller of the soil in a fixed home, living on the products of his own labor. It is only when he reaches this last step that he can be classed as civilized.

All of the religions have had their birth with man in his first or second stage; for man, when civilized, accounts for the various phenomena of nature on scientific principles, and thereby has no occasion to attribute such things to unknown beings.

Moses and the Exodus

This brings us to the time or epoch when the name of Moses and the exodus appear on the scene of Hebrew mythology. And here the question is presented, Was Moses a real character, and the exodus a fact? or was it a mere fiction? It has been contended by writers whose statements are worthy of serious consideration, that Moses had no real existence. The Rev. A. H. Sayce, the archaeologist, in his work entitled "Records of the Past," speaking of the Sun God of Chaldean mythology, says: "We learn from a Babylonian text, recently discovered in upper Egypt, that his (Moses') title was Mosu, the hero, a word which is letter for letter the same as the Hebrew Moshoh." He further says that this name dates back to Accadian cosmology, where Mosu (Moses) was deified as the sun God. The learned Huet, Vossius, Clark, and other writers give a long list of parallel acts of Moses and the Egyptian Bacchus, and

21

assert that they were one and the same, and that the mythical Bacchus was the one.

While Renan thinks that Moses had a real existence, he says: "The man has been buried beneath the legends that have grown up around him, until his real character is lost in an ocean of myths." This author says that no writings have been found concerning Moses which can be traced back to within 500 years after his death; that, according to the Thora, Moses led his men against the Moabites; but that, in the Book of Wars of Iahveh, he had disappeared before reaching this people.

Manetho, in his Egyptian history, gives Moses a personal existence, and informs us that the man's real name was Osarsiph, which was changed to Moses at the time he took his people out of Egypt.

These authorities can be reconciled only on the hypothesis that the name Moses had a place, not only among the Gods of Chaldea, but also with the celestial beings of Egypt. Assuming such to be the case, this man had a reason for casting off the name of Osarsiph and assuming that of Moses, as he thereby became the divine ruler of his people; for a man who could successfully lead his people out of Egypt would find it an easy task to convince them that he was of divine origin. Times then were easy, when Gods were created with little difficulty, and with as little effort the multitude were induced to render homage.

Josephus says, "Moses was appointed general, and with his army drove the Ethiopians out of Egypt;" but we must remember that Josephus derived most of his information concerning Moses from Hebrew legends. We are told in biblical records that Moses, after being permitted to leave the country, gathered up the Israelites, 600,000 men, besides the women and children, and with so vast a horde marched to the Red Sea, where with a small rod he divided the waters of that sea and passed through, and that the whole Egyptian army, attempting to follow them, was swallowed up. This is a remarkable story, hardly able to stand alone, when we take into consideration the fact that, at that time, the Egyptians kept full accounts of their wars and all other important events of their country, and that there has never been found among the records or traditions of that people as much as a mention of the loss of the Egyptian army in the Red Sea. The biblical statement stands without support. All of this, when taken in connection with the Mosaic exploits at Mount Sinai, and the numerous conversations, contracts, covenants, oaths, and conspiracies between him and Jehovah, as reported in the Hebrew writing, seems to warrant the conclusion that the whole record of his exploits is but a myth. Such were the teachings of the Rabbinical schools of Canaan 500 years after Moses' death. The biblical story of Moses' birth, that he was placed in a basket of rushes, put on the Nile, where he was picked up, and reared in the king's family, is so much like the Chaldean story and legend told of Sargon, who ruled Assyria 1600 B. C, that one can readily believe the former was borrowed by the author of the Hebrew account from the latter story.

The Chaldean inscriptions, wherein Sargon tells his own story, read as follows: "My mother was a princess; my father I did not know (nor did Moses). My mother placed me in an ark of rushes, with bitumen; my exit she sealed up. She launched me on the river (Euphrates), which did not drown me. The river carried me to Akki; the water it brought me. Akki, the water-carrier, in tenderness of bowels lifted me. Akki, the water-carrier, as his child brought me up. Akki, the water-carrier, as his husbandman placed me."

Sargon was an usurper, and ruled forty-five years. All of these things belong to the age of fables and myths. There are also other circumstances in support of this theory, of too much significance to be overlooked. If Moses was a man of so much importance as the Hebrew writings make him to appear, it is hardly possible, or, at least, it is not probable, that he would have so suddenly and unceremoniously dropped out of sight and forever disappeared from history, after his Mount Sinai exploits, that the time, place, and manner of his death and burial should ever remain unknown. History does not deal in this way with great men; it follows them in detail down to the last moment of their lives, and then buries them amid the pomp and splendor of the multitude.

The Hebrews from the Time They Went into Egypt Until the Captivity

The Hyksos. — A history of the departure of the children of Israel from Egypt would be hardly complete without some mention of the Hyksos, or Shepherd Kings, as they were called, who were so closely allied to the Hebrews in peace, in war, and in religion. Whether the Hyksos originally belonged to Arabia, Syria, Mesopotamia, or Bactria, are questions which must ever remain in doubt. Different authors have expressed diverse opinions on this point, all of which have been mere conjecture, as there is little or no direct evidence on the point, beyond the character and features of that people; but this much can, with reasonable certainty, be said of them, that they belonged to the Semitic branch of the Turanian family, or stock, and were monotheists. It is somewhat uncertain whether at an early date they were not a branch of the Hebrews. Josephus leans strongly to that opinion. When the Hyksos immigrated to Egypt is uncertain, but it must have been from two to four centuries before the first stock of Hebrews settled in that country, for on the entrance of the first division of the Hebrews into the delta, they found the Hyksos, not only settled in large numbers, but in full power in both lower and upper Egypt. It was the Shepherd Kings, or Pharaohs, who permitted the Hebrews to settle there. Maiielho, an Egyptian high priest, and reliable historian, who wrote the history of Egypt from the time of Menu, the first king, down to his time, about the middle of the third century B. C, in speaking of the Hyksos, says that during the reign of Timaus, there came an invasion from the east, men of ignoble birth, who subdued the Egyptians, and set up a king of their own, whom they called Salatis, who made Memphis his home; that he rebuilt and fortified Avaris, and that he and his descendants ruled the country five hundred and eleven years; that at the end of this time, upper and lower Egypt revolted, and with a great army, and after a long war, finally shut up the Hyksos in Avaris; that Timaus, not being able to take the city by force, allowed the Hyksos to take their families and depart; that they went into Syria and built a city which they called Jerusalem. It may be said here that there is nothing running counter to this statement of Manetho that the Elyksos built that city. The town was originally called Salem, and went by that name until the conquest of Canaan, when it fell into the hands of the Jews, after which it was called the Salem of the Jews, or Jews' Salem, and finally corrupted into Jerusalem.

The Hebrews in Egypt

At the risk of a little repetition, let it be said that the Hebrews went into Egypt from the land of Canaan in at least two divisions, and some considerable distance of time between them. The first installment, led by the Abramites, consisted of a small party, and some time thereafter a much larger body of Israelites entered Egypt and were assigned lands in the delta for themselves and their herds, for they were shepherds or herdsmen like the Hyksos, and were equally despised by the Egyptians, who looked on the roaming life of such people with contempt. The Hebrews were low and ignorant, forming a wide contrast to the highly civilized, cultivated, and refined Egyptians. It is no wonder that such a cultivated people looked down with contempt on a lot of herdsmen, a little above their cattle in the scale of advancement, but the Egyptians were not in power; as before stated, the country was under the dominion of the Hyksos, who, if they did not invite the Hebrews into the country, received them with open arms as friends and fellow-worshipers of a single deity.

The Sojourn of the Hebrews in Egypt

As before stated, the duration of the sojourn of the children of Israel in the land of the Pharaohs will never be settled, as there is a great diversity of opinion.

Perhaps it may be safely said that a majority of the writers, basing their opinions on the genealogical table of the Levites, have fixed the sojourn at about two hundred and fifteen years, but they do not make this claim with much degree of certainty, owing to the dearth of evidence in support of their opinion. Bunsen, after a thorough research, concludes that they must have been in Egypt as much as fourteen centuries, and that they left the country in the reign of Menephthah, about 1320 or 1314 B. C. This author assumed, on the statements of the writer of the Torah, that the fighting force of the Hebrews at the time of their exit was 600,000, to which add the old and the young and the women, and we have from two and a half to three millions, which is believed by many writers to be about the number who left the country. On this assumption Bunsen concludes that it would take at least fourteen centuries of natural increase to make this number, and this is the only reason put forth by him on which to base his conclusion. In order to agree with this author, we should be forced to accept his major premises, which we think to be unwarranted, in view of the well-known fact that the number who went into the country is unknown.

The time when, Bunsen says, the Hebrews left the country, 1320 or 1314, agrees with the time stated by Manetho when they were driven out. The writer of Exodus (believed to be Ezra) says that the sojourn of the children of Israel in Egypt was 430 years, adding that they left the land the selfsame day on which they entered it. These two statements, so flatly contradicting each other, will hardly be taken as much authority, and if the author is no more reliable in other matters than in this, his statement that the Red Sea, at the command of Moses, opened up to allow his people to pass through, and then closed in on the Egyptian army, should receive little or no consideration whatever.

As it required the suspension of a law of nature to work this alleged miracle, the intelligent reader of to-day will be inclined to reject the entire story as a fact, and assign to it a place among fables and myths. In the days of Josephus, even, the more enlightened Jews treated the miraculous part of the story with contempt, while it has become quite the fashion among the more advanced Christians of this time to explain away the miracle, by asserting that the exit was across the marshes at the north end of the sea. This miracle has its parallel in the statement, just as well authenticated, that the Pamphylian Sea opened at the command of Alexander to allow his army to cross it. Take away the miracle of the Red Sea, and with it falls the whole exodus story as told by its author, thereby leaving the children of Israel in the land of the Pharaohs, their exit to be explained in other ways.

Manetho here comes to the rescue, with the only reasonable and plausible version of the problem, in which he is supported in both a negative and positive manner by the records of the country. It will be remembered that, as a historian of the third century B. C, he had access to all the records of Egypt.

Before giving the statements of Manetho, it will be first in order of time to briefly sketch the opinions of a few of the numerous writers who have so laboriously delved into the question, to learn how wide and diverse their opinions are on the same subject-matter. If it were true, it would seem that there should be no difference of opinion. If the exodus, as described in that book, be true, why there should be such a diversity of opinion as to the time of the occurrence of so important an event is a question that will be asked by all inquiring minds, to which there can be no ready answer. Following are the opinions of some of the numerous authors:

Usher says, 'The exodus took place 1491 B.C.;" Hale says, 1648; Wilkinson fixes 1495 in the reign of Thothmes III; Bunsen says 1320 to 1314, in the reign of Menephtah; Prof. Lepsius gives the latter part of the 19th dynasty; others run the dates from 2019 to 1300 B. C, and assert that the number of Hebrews that went out was about 3,250,000.

Brugsch, in his "Egypt Under the Pharaohs," agrees with Bunsen that Menephtah was the Pharaoh of the exodus, succeeded by Seti II, who was followed by Menephtah III.

Maspero, a French author, places the exodus under Seti II., and says that during the 18th and 19th dynasties, monumental and papyrus-roll history was kept all over Egypt.

Under Seti I and Rameses II, it is claimed that the Hebrews were oppressed.

Josephus says the Hebrews went out of Egypt under the reign of Tethmosis, rendered by some Tethmus, by others, Ahmos or Amos, thus agreeing with Africanus, who says they went out under the reign of Amos.

Some other writers do not agree with this, but assert that it was during the reign of Amos that the Hyksos went out. This cannot be correct, unless we admit that Amos was a monarch of the 17th dynasty, which has no evidence in its support, but on the contrary it appears that Amos belonged to the latter part of the 18th or the early part of the 19th dynasty.

It may be said with propriety that much of the confusion here arises out of imperfect knowledge of rendering names, and the fact that dates under the chronological system of Egypt commence de novo with each Pharaoh. For instance, Thutmus is by Josephus rendered Tethmosis; by Africanus, it is Amos, and by Eusebius, it is Amosis.

McDonald, in his chronology, makes Thutmus I reign 1356; Thutmus III 1341; Ahmos, 1396; Amenhotep, 1371; and Rameses, 1333 B. C. These dates fall within the 18th and 19th dynasties.

Menephtah was on the throne about 131 5 B. C. During his reign the country was invaded from the south by the Libyans, and at the same time by an African prince named Marmaiu, with a force of 30,000 warriors collected from five nations; joined to this force came a fleet of 10,000 mariners from Greece, Italy, and Asia Minor. After a desperate struggle the invaders were driven out of the country. This, says an historian, is the first marine war recorded in history. Full and complete accounts of it have been found on Egyptian monuments. It is claimed by several writers that the exodus took place almost immediately after this war. If, as stated in the Hebrew records, the Egyptian army was, in following the Jews, swallowed up in the Red Sea, it was a matter of too much importance to have escaped the chroniclers of that time, hence should have a place on the monuments.

The exit of the Hebrews, according to the foregoing authorities, took place during the 18th or 19th dynasty, and probably not far from 1320 B.C. As to the evidence on this point, we have the statements as to the time of the exit, by the above authors, founded on the assumption that the event, as described by the author of the book of Exodus, was an established fact, leaving the question as to the truth of that statement untouched. It is the truth or falsity of that statement that is now at issue. On the one side we have the naked, unsupported statement or assertion of the author of the Hebrew Torah, the Greek Pentateuch, who is undoubtedly Ezra and his assistants, and his story founded on a miracle, handed down by tradition for nearly ten centuries before being reduced to writing. On the other side we have the negative and positive records of Egypt, and the history of Manetho, founded on a natural state of things. Ezra wrote his version, as we shall show further on, nearly a thousand years after the alleged event, and by his own statement it was written from memory; while Manetho had the records of Egypt from which to write.

It may be safely said that the 18th and 19th dynasties cover the most brilliant and prosperous period in Egyptian history. In point of learning the Egyptians were in advance of any former or subsequent age in their history.

Ferguson, the Egyptologist and historian, says the 18th, 19th, and 20th dynasties cover the most brilliant period in Egyptian annals, i.e., that at no other time did the Egyptian chroniclers furnish so full and complete narratives of every event happening in their country. This author further says: "In refinement, learning, architecture, and luxuries, she had reached the pinnacle of fame; the writings included history, divinity, philosophy, correspondence, travels, novels, and legends."

We might quote to the same purport from other authors, but as this is undisputed, further evidence is uncalled for. In point of architecture, Rawlinson, the great historian, says: "The hall of Seti at Karnak is the greatest of man's architectural works, and the building to which it belongs is the noblest ever produced by the hand of man." Another writer says: "The architectures of Greece and Rome sink into insignificance as compared with that of Egypt."

The monumental inscriptions and papyrus rolls, comprising the records of that wonderful people, have survived the elements of centuries, come down to our time, and been recently unearthed and deciphered.

If the exodus, as described in the Pentateuch, had taken place as therein stated, and. the army of Egypt, while pursuing the Israelites, had been swallowed up in the waters of the Red Sea, is it possible that the records would have been silent on so disastrous a matter? The event would have been of too much importance to have been overlooked, especially when the laws of nature had to be suspended in order to accomplish the salvation of the Israelites. It would seem that there can be but one answer to that question. Sir William Osburn, a thorough Egyptologist and hieroglyphist, after spending thirty years among the tombs, monuments, and ruins of Egypt, and having specially searched to find recorded evidence of the Hebrews, says, in his "Monumental History of Egypt," that he has failed to find any mention, or trace of any kind, bearing on or tending to sustain the biblical account of the exodus. We can hardly forbear quoting from Chevalier Bunsen, one of the ablest Egyptologists, who, in speaking of the biblical story of the exodus, says: "The barriers which Jewish superstition and Christian sloth have erected in the field of history, are forever broken down. Historical records and truth cannot be destroyed by the preposterous claims advanced by the clergy to fabricate history in order to bring us back to the dark ages."

While it cannot in justice be claimed that the silence of the Egyptian records is conclusive proof against the Hebrew story of the exodus, we think it must in all fairness be admitted that it throws a cloud over that story.

If the matter rested here, the story of the exodus as told by Ezra would remain an unsolved problem. But truth here comes to the rescue, with a smile on its face, and introduces the reader to the great Egyptian historian, Manetho, and asks him, in his "History of Egypt," to tell us how Moses and the children of Israel got out of the land of the Pharaohs. Hear what he has to say. Manetho says: "Amenophis (who was then on the throne) consulted the Gods as to how to get rid of the Hebrews. The advice was to drive them out of Egypt. The Hebrews asked the king that they be allowed to depart; the king refused to grant their request, but sent them into the stone quarries; afterward, at their request, he allowed them to occupy Avaris, which had been desolate since the departure of the shepherds; among them there were several learned priests afflicted with leprosy; one of them, named Osarsiph, a priest of Heliopolis, they made their ruler; having fortified the city, Osarsiph incited an insurrection against Amenophis, and sent to Jerusalem, to the formerly expelled shepherds, for aid; they responded with alacrity, and came to the assistance of Osarsiph, whose name was afterward changed to Moses."

So far the statements of Manetho substantially agree with the Hebrew account. Manetho further says: "Amenophis, with his army, was compelled to flee into Ethiopia." This point is in substance supported by Josephus. Manetho then proceeds to say: "The Egyptians remained in Ethiopia for thirteen years; during this time Osarsiph burned the towns and destroyed the images of the Gods; after the thirteen years Amenophis returned to Egypt with a great army and drove these leprous and unclean people and their allies out of Egypt, to the borders of Syria."

Leaving out the Red Sea miracle and some minor details, the two accounts are not in substantial conflict. The Hebrews, finding themselves pushed to the borders of Syria, had to do one of two things: fight their way through the nation of Philistines, or turn back to the southeast of Mount Sinai. Josephus comes to our aid here, and says the Hebrews did attempt to pass through the Philistines and were driven back.

Here apply the statements of the author of Exodus, who finds them at the base of Mount Sinai, and the whole story of the exit is told without the intervention of a miracle, which was undoubtedly added by Ezra to embellish and round off the tale for the edification of the children of Israel, and make them believe that Jehovah was their protector. It may here be said that the monumental inscriptions recently brought to light in Egypt fully sustain the historical accounts given by Manetho.

The Hebrews at Mount Sinai were among their friends and in a country where they could procure food and water for themselves until such time as they could get ready to pass around that mount to the east of the Jordan and so enter the land of Canaan. The length of time which the Hebrews remained at Mount Sinai and on the desert of Paran must ever remain in doubt, for notwithstanding the Hebrew statement of forty years, no record of them is given beyond the first two years, during which, it is said, full details of their doings have been supplied. Goethe says that the period of forty years was but a mythical round number; that the real time was two years. Three, seven, twelve, and forty were favorite numbers among all the pagan nations, from whom they were undoubtedly borrowed by the Hebrews, and later by the Christians. The forty days of the flood, forty years in the wilderness, forty days on Mount Sinai, and the forty days of fasting are but borrowed myths.

Renan says that the number of Hebrews who left Egypt must have been very small, as the desert country around Sinai is such that but a few people could have found support there; that at the present time the country is peopled with a few hundred half-starved Bedouins.

Before proceeding to consider the exploits of Moses at Mount Sinai, let it be remembered that the Hebrew populace had, in spite of their priests, during their long stay in Egypt, accepted the religion of that country, to which they adhered up to the time of their release from Babylonian captivity, worshiping Horus, Ra, Turn, Aten, Apis, and other Egyptian divinities, in common with the principal divinities of Canaan.

Moses and some of the other learned priests, while in Egypt, cast off Elohim, the plural of Anu, El, and Hea, and in its place substituted the name Iahveh, afterward written Jahveh, or Jehovah; that is, they exchanged the pagan divinity of the Chaldeans for the pagan divinity of the Egyptians. In proof of this we cite Williamson, who, in his "History of Israel," says: "That Elohim was the divine name used by the Hebrews up to the time of Moses; that Iahveh, or Jehovah, was the sacred name used by the Egyptian priests, has been proven from monumental inscriptions, and by Spencer, Marsham, Jabonski, Skinner, and other Egyptologists."

Jehovah and the Hebrew Ritual Borrowed from Egypt

As a foundation or preliminary to this branch of the discussion, we quote from Rawlinson, who says that Amenhotep IV attempted to restore, in a modified form, the religion which Apepi had endeavored to institute, the worship of Aten, the sun God. Apepi attempted to turn the people from the worship of all the Gods except Set; that name being familiar to the people, he preferred it to Iahveh, or Jehovah, which had been used by the priests from early times. The followers of Amenhotep were called disk worshipers. This author further says that the. forms of worship set up by the Israelites in the desert were the same as those of the disk worshipers, and that the sacred furniture and shewbread described in Exodus are the same as used in the worship of Aten. The God Aten being looked upon by the Egyptian populace as the physical sun, as such they worshiped that orb.

The Egyptians, like most other pagan nations, had their trinities; the sun, being one of them, rose as Horus, shone in mid-heavens as Ra, and set as Tum. These divinities were recognized as the three vital qualities and attributes centering in one supreme head, called by the priests Jehovah, the personification of the great solar orb. The Jehovah, sometimes represented as "I am," in Exodus, is the same as "I am all that is," which has been found on the Egyptian monuments.

From what has been here shown, there can be no doubt about the fact that Jehovah, the God of the Hebrews and Christians, is but a pagan deity borrowed from Egypt, whose pedigree runs back to Chaldea, to Elam, and to the city of Ur (the birthplace of the mythical Abraham), where he was adored as the great solar disk. This same divinity, first represented by the sun, has occupied one and three places, as one and three beings, all along the pagan line from 4000 years B. C. to the present time.

In Elam and Chaldea he, as a trinity, was Anu, El, and Hea, united in Elohim; in India he is Brahma, Vishnu, and Siva, united in Trimurti; in Persia he is Ahura, Gema, and Sosiosh, united in Ahura-Mazda; in Egypt he is Horus, Ra, and Tum, united in Jehovah; in Greece he is Osiris, Isis, and Orus, united in Zeus; in Scandinavia he is Odin, Vila, and Ve, united in Hel; with the Christians he is Father, Son, and Ghost, united in Jehovah.

Moses at Mount Sinai

The next that is heard of Moses and his people, according to biblical records, is at Mount Sinai. On the acts and doings at this place and epoch rest Hebrew and Christian mythology.

Mount Sinai, nearly 9,000 feet high, is the loftiest, most forbidding, and most desolate mountain in southwestern Asia. From base to summit it is destitute of vegetation; its formation is principally dark granite; its summit is often covered with glistening ice and snow; terrible storms gather around it; the thunder echoes at its base, while the lightning exposes to view its solitude. When all is quiet, the awful silence of its desolation is appalling; the traveler, Josephus informs us, was afraid to stop there to feed his stock; he shuddered at the very sound of his own footsteps. The Babylonians looked upon this mountain as the home of Anu, El, and Hea; and the children of Israel as the home of Elohim and Jehovah.

The biblical writings represent the God of Israel on this mountain, surrounded by angels, riding on the wings of the wind and flames of fire, speaking in tones of thunder, and rending the cloudy veil to show himself in the lightning.

It is no wonder that Moses, in his flight from Egypt, selected this mountain as the place to talk with and procure from Jehovah a code of laws for the government of the people of Israel. Here Moses met Jehovah in his own home, while the credulous, simple Hebrews consented to wait at the foot of the mountain until their hero went up for the laws and commandments; for they were afraid of this desolate mountain and the wrath of its monarch.

Moses and his Laws

Now let us proceed to the discussion of the character of Moses and the sacred laws and commandments contained in the five books ascribed to him.

On these writings, and their supposed divine authorship, hang the Hebrew and Christian religions. The Hebrews and Christians have been taught to believe, and they have believed as they were taught by their priests, that Moses wrote these laws at the command of Jehovah, or that Jehovah wrote them at the command of Moses, and that Moses brought these writings down out of Mount Sinai, put them in an ark where they were safely kept, and that they have been correctly translated into the various languages of Christendom.

Now, if this be true, then these laws ought to be, not only good authority, but binding and conclusive on all of the world. On the other hand, if Moses did not get them in this way, or get them at all, but they were the writings of man, or men, as mere ordinary mortals, and were written long after the death of Moses, then they have, and of right should have, no force or effect whatever. Now, these are the questions which we propose to discuss.

So far as the writings go, on their face, they, we believe, purport to come through Moses. The writings recite, or inform us, that while in the wilderness the followers of Moses became disheartened, and insisted on returning to Egypt; that they had become so clamorous that Moses, to appease them, promised that, if they would wait at the foot of the mountain, he would have a conference with Jehovah, and he assured his people that Jehovah had often promised to conduct them safely out of the desert and into the land of Canaan. But they had become weary and disheartened, and refused to believe Moses, or to believe that his God was in the mountain at all. Moses finally persuaded them to wait at the foot of the mountain, when, according to the Bible, he took with him Aaron, Nadab, and Abihu, and seventy elders, making seventy-four in all, seventy-three exclusive of himself. When part the way up the mountain Jehovah appeared before them standing on a sapphire stone, and all the seventy-four saw him. After this Moses proceeded alone up into the mountain, waited six days, got the laws from Jehovah, stayed forty days longer, and then returned with the laws written or engraved on tablets of stone.

Now, to say the least of it, this is a remarkable story, apparently contrary to natural laws, and contrary to all our experience, and it rests on the statement of Moses, unsupported by a single witness; for not one of the seventy-three others has been produced or has offered to come forward to say one word in corroboration of the statement of Moses. The statement of Moses that the

31

other seventy-three persons saw Jehovah, is not their statement, but his alone. Moses must have known that this statement was an unnatural one, and that his people would require all the evidence possible in its support, then why did he not call some one or all of the seventy-three persons to vouch in some way or manner for his story? The fact that he did not do so, or attempt to do so, would be, in this age of the world, conclusive evidence of the untruthfulness of the statement, even if made by a man of the highest character for truth and integrity. In this case Moses has not even this to back him, for according to the same authority, he was guilty of willful murder in Egypt, and also of entering into a conspiracy to cheat and defraud the Egyptian women of their jewelry.

Even the followers of Moses did not believe his Mount Sinai story, for Aaron, while his brother was up in the mountain, set up a golden calf, the Apis bull of Egypt; and while in the desert the Hebrews continued the worship of the Egyptian divinities, notwithstanding the exertions of the priests to turn them over to Jehovah.

This continuous religious warfare between the priests and the populace did not cease on their return to Canaan; they had lost the numerous Egyptian deities, and refused to accept Jehovah or the teachings of Moses and the other priests; nor was it until the close of the Babylonian captivity that the priests, under the leadership of Ezra and Nehemiah, were able, in that land of captivity, to bring the Hebrews back to a quasi recognition of the power of Jehovah, as manifested through the priests of his chosen people.

Contrary to the general belief of seventy years of captivity, the records show but fifty, and this is the time now agreed on by numerous writers. It is conceded that Jerusalem was destroyed and that the people were carried off by Nebuchadnezzar in the year 586 B.C. Cyrus, the Persian monarch, overthrew Babylon in the year 536 B.C, and no later than the following year the Jews were released, when, it is said, some 40,000 of them, with some Levite priests, returned to Jerusalem.

This argument is based on the theory that these sacred laws and commandments were of Mosaic origin. We do not propose to stop here, but to proceed and prove that neither of these five books, nor any part of the Old Testament writings, came from Closes or from Jehovah, and that neither Moses nor Jehovah ever saw or heard of these writings; in short, that Moses left no writings whatever at the time of his death, but that the five books comprising the Hebrew Thora, or Greek Pentateuch, generally ascribed to Moses, were written nearly a thousand years after his death.

It is said that Moses brought from Mount Sinai an ark, meaning a box, containing at least the ten commandments engraved on tablets. Biblical records assert that he carried this ark around in his nomadic wanderings and in his marauding expeditions; but there is no evidence that anyone ever saw the inside of that box, or ever heard what became of its contents. An able Egyptologist says that the Hebrews had no alphabet up to the time of their return to Canaan; that Moses could not have written the Pentateuch in Egyptian characters, they being too unwieldy for so extensive a work, hence he could not have been the author of those books. As to the laws of Moses, Brugsch, in his "History of Egypt," says that the author of the Pentateuch, in compiling his code of laws, did but translate into Hebrew the religious precepts that he found in Egypt.

Origin of the Books of Moses and Other Sacred Writings of the Hebrews

We have now reached the point as to the origin of the five books generally ascribed to Moses.

This subject has been ably and thoroughly examined and discussed by numerous scholars and historians of every shade of opinion, from the radical Christian to the most ultra skeptic. In some of the minor details there is quite a diversity of opinion, some maintaining that the five books were written in whole and taken from tradition at the Babylonian captivity; while others assert that Moses and the early Hebrews left the substance of these books in different manuscripts; and still others assert that they were made up partly from fragmentary writings and traditions. But all of these authors agree that at least the first four books of the Pentateuch, and probably the fifth, in their present form, were first made known and published in the world by Ezra and Nehemiah, about 445 B. C, nearly 1,000 years after Moses.

The Rev. McClintock, the writer in "Cyclopedia of B. & E. L.," says that the authenticity of the Pentateuch was first called in question earl in the second century by the author of the "Clementine Homilies," who claimed that the law was given early to Moses, and reduced to writing after his death. Jerome denied it to be the work of Moses. Aben Ezra, of the Royal College of Paris, expressed a similar opinion. Astruc, a professor in that school, was the first who discovered in the Pentateuch two distinct documents, the Elohist and the Jehovist. Spinoza disputed its generally accepted authorship, and attributed it in its present form to Ezra. A. T. Hartmann, in his criticisms, maintains that the Pentateuch was made up of numerous fragments thrown loosely together. A majority of the critics agree that it was composed of traditions and of numerous writings originating between the time of David or Josiah and the Babylonian captivity.

Well might the Rev. McClintock exclaim: "The language of Christ and his apostles is such that the hypothesis of the Pentateuch not being the work of Moses must create a very painful feeling in the mind of every true and simple-hearted follower of Christ." In this opinion we most heartily concur, for, according to the four gospels, Christ and his apostles numerous times were made to assert, directly and by way of assumption, that Moses was the author of the Pentateuch. But this is not all, for all of the Hebrew and Christian writers and teachers have proclaimed the same thing until quite recently, when criticism commenced its work of dissecting the authorship. What position does this place Christ and his disciples in? Certainly in no other than their ignorance of a state of facts discovered by other men on examination of the books themselves; not very complimentary on the intelligence of a God and his inspired apostles. Dr. Davidson, in his "Introduction to the Old Testament," in speaking of the five books ascribed to Moses, says: "There is little external evidence for the Mosaic authorship, and what little there is does not stand the test of criticism." He further says: "The succeeding writers of the Old Testament do not confirm it; the objections derived from internal structure are conclusive against the Mosaic authorship; various contradictions are irreconcilable; the traces of a later date are convincing." He further says: "The narratives of the Pentateuch are partly mythical and legendary. The miracles recorded are the exaggerations of a later age. Moses was not the first writer who penned parts of the national legends and history."

Chambers says: "The early claims of Mosaic authorship of the Pentateuch have been generally abandoned." In this the latest authors concur.

After Babylon had been captured by Cyrus, the Persian king, one of the first acts of this monarch was to issue an edict releasing the Jews from captivity, and permitting such of them as so desired, to return to Jerusalem. It is claimed that about 40,000 of them at once availed themselves of this privilege; but where did these 40,000 come from? The Hebrews had been in captivity but fifty years, and the total number of captives taken from Jerusalem at the two sieges did not exceed 3,000. A few years thereafter, Ezra and Nehemiah, accompanied by several elders, proceeded to Jerusalem, carrying with them the entire writings comprising the Pentateuch and other sacred writings, and called together all the Israelites, when Ezra and Nehemiah occupied several days in reading these so-called Mosaic laws and commandments, including the account of the creation of the world, the fall of Adam, the flood, etc. After this reading, all the Hebrews took an oath to believe and obey these books as the works of Moses.

Ezra ought to be good authority on this subject. He says, or is made to say, that he and others wrote these books during the Babylonian captivity. He further says, that all of the sacred writings of the Jews had been burned, and that he had undertaken to write all that had been done in the world from the beginning, and that he wrote from memory.

Renan, in his third volume of "Israel," insists, with much force of argument and some evidence, that the generally accepted opinion derived from three of the early fathers of the church, that Ezra wrote the whole of the Thora at Babylon from memory, cannot be maintained; he asserts that at the time of the destruction of the temple at the second siege of Jerusalem by Nebuchadnezzar, the Hebrews carried with them into captivity fragments of the sacred writings, including the Thora, in an unfinished condition, and that from these fragments, and from memory, the Thora and other scriptures were made.

Whatever sacred writings the Hebrews then possessed were undoubtedly in the temple. There were no copies, for copying at that time among that people was not in vogue; nor did the common people, who could not read, know anything about these writings except through the teachings of the priests; and they cared less, for they worshiped the pagan divinities around them, recognizing Iahveh only when forced to do so by the priests.

History informs us that, at the first siege, all of the priests and other leading men were carried off, and that, at the second siege, when the temple was destroyed, there were none but the common people to carry into Babylon, who took no stock in these writings. Which ever version be true, the main fact that Moses did not write any of these books, and that even the fragments from which they were compiled or written had no existence for more than 500 years after Moses' death, stands out as conclusive against the alleged authorship by Moses. When a people migrate from one country to another, they carry with them the things which to them are the most valuable and sacred.

To these people their most valuable and sacred things were their Gods, their religion, and their household utensils. The traditions of the Chaldeans concerning the creation and the flood were household words with the priesthood of Israel during all of the long period from their exit from Ur until the reign of David, when these writings were commenced; and, at least so far as the Pentateuch, the history of Moses, and some other writings are concerned, they were reduced to their present form during the Babylonian captivity, by Ezra et al.

At the time of Ezra's writing these legends of creation, of Adam and Eve, of the garden and of the flood, they were already in second copy in the archives of Babylon, where Ezra undoubtedly had access to them to aid him in making up the books he carried back to Jerusalem. If Ezra palmed off on his less intelligent and confiding followers these mythical legends, as coming from Jehovah, or from Moses, it was only one among the numerous religious frauds of his time.

We will now offer in evidence some further proof of the authorship of these books. Renan informs us that the Hebrews possessed no writings up to the time of David; that the history of that people prior to that time rested on tradition; that during the reign of David and Solomon (about seventy years) some scraps of sacred history were written. Some sketches comprising the framework of the Pentateuch were made up from old Babylonian legends. It is quite apparent that at least a part of the tenth chapter of Genesis dates from Solomon's reign; that among the writings at this time appeared the legends of Chaldea and the mythical Abraham, also the life of Moses, but there are found no writings relating to the exploits of Moses at Sinai; that the writings comprised in the Pentateuch, as purporting to have come from Jehovah on Mount Sinai, are of much later origin. The author says: "The populace, being mere children, were much edified by these stories; Christianity having restored a second childhood, the gospels were well adapted to fill the vacuum." In speaking of the oracles, the same author says: "Divine manifestations were made principally through the prophets, this device having supplanted the old enigmatical machine, which replied Urim and Thummim. This device, or machine, worked on the rule of chance, like the throwing of dice, giving the answer in the affirmative or negative as the manifestation of the divine will." This author further says: "It was believed that Iahveh, having become disgusted with the machine plan, thought it more in keeping with his dignity and with the progress of the times to be heard through a class of men called prophets."

Sacred history teaches us that all Gods are progressive, and inclined to keep pace with civilization when not held in check by their priests. As to this matter, Renan says: "Progress in religion may be made in two ways, either by directly attacking a bad creed, by destroying or suppressing unworthy Gods, or by improving the special God, without changing his name, by gradually raising him to the type of an universal divinity." In this way, this author says, "Jehovah became the absolute God, and the fatal name Iahveh was suppressed by declaring it unpronounceable; that an idol, a false God, if there ever was one, has become through the steady action of an intense volition of the Hebrews, the only true God."

In further speaking of the Hebrew writings, Renan tells us: "The life of Elijah, like the life of Christ, was particularly prolific in legends; Elijah and Isaac furnished the basis of Jewish, Christian, and Mussulman mythology; they were the great divine agents of Messiahism, the forerunner of celestial apparitions; and Elijah, like Christ, spent forty days in reaching Mount Horeb, where he beheld visions resembling those of Moses at Mount Sinai; the foundation for the legends attributed to Moses had undoubtedly been reduced to writing by Elijah, or at least in his time; and Elijah and Elisha belong entirely to legends; the prophetism of the north not only created Elijah, it also created Moses, and the sacred history of Moses and the Thora were the starting-point for both Judaism and Christianity." The author further says: "The substance of the legends concerning the creation, of Adam and Eve, and of Moses, appear in the patriarchal legends and in the Book of the Wars of Iahveh, but as writing was at that date little in use, and unknown to the populace, they remained content to rest on tradition." The discrepancies and contradictions in the sacred books are the result of different minds reading tradition in different ways.

As to the Elohist and Jehovist versions, this author says: "It is evident that they were written by two or more persons, the former at the north, the latter at Jerusalem; that the original documents did not bear the signatures of their authors; that on inspection it is apparent that the different authors did not act in concert, and that an attempted blending was thereafter made by other persons, who attempted to retain the whole of the different versions, to do which, it was found impossible to make them harmonize. Hence the jars, conflicts, and absurdities."

This author says there is evidence that this first attempt to harmonize and compile took place in the time of Hezekiah and under his supervision (about 825 or 800 B.C.); Hezekiah removed many useless repetitions, condensed and pruned ad libitum.

Renan further informs us that while the two kingdoms, Israel and Judah, held many traditions in common, nevertheless after their separation under Rehoboam Jerusalem had documents unknown to Israel; that neither the Elohist nor the Jehovist contained a developed Thora; that the decalogue was written at Jerusalem, while the books of the covenant were written at the north; that at this time, and probably as the result of this compilation, Iahveh and Elohim became merged in one, the Jehovah of the Hebrews and Christians. We learn that the book of David was written not earlier than the captivity; some assert as late as 175 B.C. The book of Enoch, says Heinrich Ewald, was written at various times between 144 and 120 B. C, and compiled in the first half century before Christ.

From this time all seems to undergo a change. Jehovah is not a new divinity; only a change of name has taken place. He is the same great solar orb of the Chaldeans and Egyptians; the same great divine being, in the form of man, who held the torch and lighted the children of Israel out of the accursed land of the Pharaohs; the same who commanded the marauding Hebrew to invade the homes of the peaceful Canaanites. Iahveh had by his intimate connection with the Hebrew priests acquired such an unenviable reputation, not only among the pagans, but with his own people, that a change became a necessity, and so, under the mild influence and the ready pen of the revisers of his divine laws, he was given the name of Jehovah, and under this appellation he soon became metamorphosed, and assumed jurisdiction over all the peoples and nations of the earth. He had turned over a new leaf; a new history was to be written; a reign of humanity was to be inaugurated; peace on earth, at least so far as this ruler was concerned, had commenced. The wars of the Israelites thereafter were their wars, in which Iahveh, now Jehovah, took no part; good-will to all mankind was the order from heaven; a new Jerusalem in which were to be gathered all the nations of the earth had by the prophets been foretold, and the new Jerusalem was to be ruled over by a descendant of the house of David, who, according to the Sadducees, was to be its political king, but according to the Pharisees, was to become a spiritual ruler. Between these two factions strife was engendered; amid the turmoil a Messiah was ushered in, a church was established, and priests were created, who took charge and assumed control over this new divinity, and led him from the path of virtue into vice. A relapse set in when Jehovah became the unwilling instrument in the hands of fiends to persecute, torture, burn, and kill those of his people who did not believe that their God had a son, and that son a virgin mother.

Under the direction of the Father and Son, war continued by the priests for more than a thousand years. When outraged humanity could endure it no longer, the people declared for a better God and a higher order of humanity. Luther and Calvin came to the rescue, but they, too, were intolerant, urging Jehovah to continue his persecutions. Then science came to the surface, and decreed all Gods to be myths.

Now let us return and make further proof as to the origin of these scriptures. Hengstenberg, in his dissertations on the Pentateuch, says that the five books bear unmistakable evidence of being the work of many authors, and written at different times; and he quotes Ezra, who says that he, with the aid of five persons, wrote these books in forty days. It will be remembered that Ezra wrote or compiled these books at Babylon, about 1,000 years after the death of Moses.

Francois Lenormant, a firm Christian, and one of the greatest archaeologists, in his work entitled, "Beginnings of History," says: "I find myself compelled to yield to evidence that the books of the Pentateuch (the Elohist and Jehovist) are not the writings of Moses, nor of any one man; the Jehovist is not the oldest, and this is now admitted among the highest English and German scholars, Protestant and Catholic. And at least the first four books of the Pentateuch, as we now have them, do not date further back than the captivity. That which we read in the first chapters of Genesis is not an account dictated by God, but it is a tradition, whose origin is lost in the night of the remotest ages, and which all of the great nations of Western Asia possessed in common, with some variations." He further says: "The very form given in the Bible is so closely related to that which has been lately discovered in Babylon and Chaldea, it follows so exactly the same course, that it is quite impossible for me to doubt any longer that it has the same origin. The family of Abraham carried this tradition with it in the migration from Ur of the Chaldees into Palestine, and even then it was doubtless already fixed in writing, or in oral form."

This author further says: "The Hebrew Genesis is from at least two distinct sources, written at different times, and by at least two persons."

It will be seen on examination that these Mosaic accounts conflict on various points; two different stories of creation are given.

The Mosaic legends of creation, the first man, his fall, the serpent, the garden of Eden, the flaming sword, and the account of the flood have their parallels. Similar legends existed from the Nile to the Indus long before the days of Moses, as will be shown further on.

The Rev. A. H. Sayce, who has devoted a great amount of time to archaeology, and especially to the Assyrio-Babylonian inscriptions, in his work entitled "Records of the Past," in speaking of the legends of creation contained in the Chaldean and Mosaic accounts, says: "In each case the history of creation is divided into seven successive acts, and the words in each case are substantially the same. The world has been preceded by a watery chaos, and the order of creation agrees in the two accounts." This is also true of the accounts given in Hindu and Persian mythology.

Draper, in his work entitled "Conflict of Science and Religion," says: "The Mosaic account of the creation and the flood was borrowed from the Chaldean legends."

The sacred writings of Zoroaster, which are at least 1,800 years older than Christ, and 400 years older than Moses, contain the accounts of the creation of the world, of the fall of man, and a flood with an ark and a saved family.

Mr. F. C. Cook, a firm Christian, in his book entitled "Origin of Religion," in comparing the account given in the book of Genesis with the account given in the Zend-Avesta, of the creation and flood, reluctantly says: "It does not matter whether these accounts were given by direct revelation to Moses, or whether the writer recorded faithfully and loyally the old traditions of the human race."

Professor Lenormant, in speaking on this subject with a view of sustaining his Christian religion, says that although the Chaldean legends from which the Mosaic account was copied were a myth, the fact that they (the old myths) were copied by inspired writers, makes the account become spiritual, and so, true. According to the reasoning of this author, the copying of a legend and myth by a Christian converts myth into truth. This is strictly in accord with Christian reasoning, i. e., a lie told by a Christian is thereby converted into a truth.

In the Cyclopaedia of Biblical, Theological, and Ecclesiastical Literature, published, in 1883, by McClintock & Strong, we are told by the pious Rev. McClintock, or, in other words, he reluctantly admits, that the Old Testament was written by Ezra and Nehemiah; and that it received accessions for many years after their death until the time of the Maccabees. He further says that the combined evidence of tradition and the general course of Jewish history lead to the conclusion that the Canon, in its present shape, was formed gradually, beginning with Ezra, and continuing through the Persian period down to 322 B. C.

If this writer had told the full truth, he would have added that there is abundant evidence showing that the Hebraic-Chaldean writings, comprising the Pentateuch and much of the other sacred writings of the Hebrews, were taken from the Chaldean legends, but, as the clergy have been engaged for more than 1,800 years in propagating a gigantic falsehood, it would be too much to expect of human nature to believe them capable of at once reversing their whole lives by telling the whole truth so recently by them learned.

Modern Judaism

The address delivered at the religious congress, at the late World's Fair, held at Chicago, by Rabbi S. H. Sonneschein, contains the modern ideas held by the Hebrews. Among other things, the speaker said: "The synagogue of to-day is undergoing great changes; it is represented by three different schools. The orthodox branch is still in Egypt, under the ban of the Talmud, which is now but a stagnant pool, a walled-in theology, feeding on the crumbs of the antiquated past. At the other extreme camps the radical school, whose leaders and followers are disciples of the modern agnostic philosophy and executors of the modern ruthless Bible criticism, with their Cod in the nebulous life-force of the cosmos, the concentrated intelligence of organized atoms and cells of natural law; with them holy writ is an antiquated literature, Abraham a myth, Moses a romance, and Judaism a phenix, which in order to live must first sacrifice itself upon the altar of self-cremation."

Origin of the Sabbath

Let it be remembered that Hebrews and Christians have ever claimed that Sunday, or, as they call it, the Sabbath, had its origin with the children of Israel. Nothing can be further from the truth. This claim of course rests on the Hebrew Bible. In the book of Exodus, xx, ii, the origin of the week of seven days is made to rest on the alleged Jehovistic story of the creation of the world; while in Deuteronomy, v, 15, the claim is made that the week, with its Sabbath, had its origin with the exodus of the Jews out of Egypt; thus raising a conflict in the claimant's own family. On this claim the Sabbath, or Sunday, has been treated as a sacred day, and its observance as such has, by custom and by law, been enforced in all Christian countries. If this claim of the Hebrews and Christians cannot be proven, then the sacred character of the day cannot be sustained. It will be observed, on further research, that the so-called Mosaic account of creation, in treating of this day, does not, even on its face, purport to establish or inaugurate the Sabbath, for it reads, "Remember the Sabbath," etc., treating it as an already established institution.

According to the latest and most reliable historical evidence we have on this subject, the Sunday, the day set apart for the worship of the sun, had its source or origin with the Accadian astrologers, more than 2,000 years before Moses. This people at that early date were not only versed in astrology, but they had some knowledge of astronomy; they recognized our solar system, the relation of the planets to each other, their revolutions, including the revolution of our earth around the sun; but they knew nothing of Uranus or Neptune. They were familiar with the legends of the creation of the world, if they were not the real authors of them.

At a later date these legends were held in common among all of the Oriental nations. As to the mythical six days of creation, and the Sunday, or day of rest, Mr. Blake, in his "History of the Heavens," says: "The Accadians, or Elamites, seem to be the authors of the legends of creation, the six days' work, and rest on the seventh; they determined the solar year, divided it into twelve months, and into weeks of seven days."

Neptune and Uranus, as before stated, not having been discovered by this people, they named the seven known planets, and called the days of the week after them: Sunday for the sun, Monday for the moon, Tuesday for Mars,

Wednesday for Mercury, Thursday for Jupiter, Friday for Venus, and Saturday for Saturn. To the six planets, as Gods, the Accadians ascribed the creation of the world, each planet performing its or his part of the work. The work having been completed on the sixth day, these planetary divinities rested on the seventh, celebrated their work, and offered up prayers and sacrifices to the sun, the greatest of all the Gods, thereby laying the foundation for keeping this day sacred in honor of the sun.

These legends, having been handed down from the Accadians to the Chaldeans, the Assyrians, and the Egyptians, were by the authors of the Thora taken from Egypt and adopted into the religious system of the Hebrews. The Egyptians having commenced their week on Sunday, their Sabbath fell on Saturday. This was strictly followed by the Hebrews.

The Brahmans adopted the same system, but commenced their week on the day of Venus, Friday.

The Hebrews and, later, the Christians, in their system of borrowing, copied the word Sabbath, which was the term used in Chaldea, Assyria, and Egypt. The Hebrews recognizing but one divine being, and having consolidated these seven divinities into one, Elohim, afterward called Jehovah, they in their borrowed legends assigned to him the whole task of creation, following the same order, using the same names, and occupying the same time as in the Accadian legends.

Strict observance of the Sabbath was enforced by the laws of Elam, Chaldea, Babylon, and Assyria thousands of years before Moses, as has been proven from the inscriptions taken out of the ruins of the cities of those countries. Cooking, washing, cleaning of clothes, offering sacrifices, riding, public speaking, cursing, and even taking medicine, were all prohibited on the Sabbath day. Apply this rule, and our clergymen would have to close their churches on Sunday.

As to borrowing this Sabbath from the pagans, Josephus, Philo, and Juleus Clemens all admit, yes, they boldly assert, that the Sabbath did not originate with the Hebrews, but that it was in common use among all the Oriental nations.

Dion Cassius, the Roman senator and historian, says: "The Egyptians were well acquainted with the true revolution of the planets, including the earth, more than 2,000 years B.C.; they divided the year into months and into weeks of seven days; named the days after the seven planets, beginning their week with Sunday. The Hebrews borrowed their week and Sabbath from the Egyptians, and so their Sabbath fell on Saturday."

As to the Christians, in the fourth century they ignored the Jewish Sabbath, and substituted the Roman Sun-day. The observance of this day having fallen into disuse, both the pagans and Christians clamored for its restoration; to appease both parties, Constantine, while yet a pagan, issued an edict in the year 321, which reads as follows: "On the venerable day of the Sun, let the magistrates and people, residing in the cities rest, and let all workshops be closed."

It will be remembered that the venerable day of the Sun was the day set apart by pagan Rome for the worship of Apollo, and called the venerable Sun-day, the day for worshiping the Sun God.

In both the original and borrowed legends, the creators got tired and rested on the seventh day, or day of the Sun. This sacred seventh day of the Accadians, as handed down to posterity, has ever been observed as a day of rest and praise of the great luminary.

As before stated, this venerable seventh day, with its observances, was adopted by the early Christians, just as received from the Jews, and was retained to the time of Constantine, who changed it from the seventh to the first day of the week in accordance with the custom of Rome; since which time the venerable day of the Sun of pagan Rome has been incorporated into the religious systems of all Christendom.

The Christian priests and clergymen are terribly in earnest in their clamor for the observance of this pagan Sunday, for it is on this venerable "Sabbath" day that 'The sly mountebank attends his trade, harangues the rabble, and is better paid."

Chaldean Legends of Creation

This brings us down to the proper place for comparing the Chaldean and Mosaic accounts of creation. The inscriptions on the Assyrio-Babylonian tablets, as found among the ruins, were so much mutilated that only parts of the legends remained perfect; but enough was found to show a story substantially like the one contained in the Mosaic records. The inscriptions on the first tablet speak of the existence of the Gods before the creation, and then say, that in the beginning all was void; that the heavens had not been raised, that the abyss had not broken its foundations. The Gods then say, *'Let there be made earth for the dwelling of man, that he may have dominion over all created things, and let the heavens be made." The account on the second, third, and fourth tablets shows that a firmament was made and called heaven; that the waters were divided from the land; that the Gods commanded the earth to bring forth all kinds of vegetation, and that each kind should produce its kind. The account on the fifth tablet says, 'The Gods arranged the stars in the heavens to shine, and they fixed the years; the moon was made to light the night; the sun to rise in the east and go in his course." The account on the sixth tablet says, "The Gods created the monsters of the sea, the beasts of the field, birds of the air, and all creeping things, and commanded each to produce after its own kind, and they were sent forth to multiply."

Then follows the creation of man, called Admi, or Adami, meaning man in general, and being used as symbolical of earth.

It will be remembered that the Mosaic account treats Adam, or speaks of him, in both characters. In some places he is spoken of as a man, or the man, while in other places in the same account he is referred to as man, mankind in

42

general. These Chaldean legends say that man was created pure; that the Gods breathed the breath of life into him, and commanded him to serve the Gods.

Then follows a command to woman to obey her husband. The account then proceeds to say that the dragon (serpent) led man to sin and to know good from evil; that in consequence of his disobedience the Gods drove him out of Canduiya, a land watered by four rivers, naming the Euphrates as one of them. The sacred grove Anu was then guarded by a sword, turned to the four points of the compass. The Gods then pronounced a curse on Admi and his issue, and threatened to destroy his seed; the diagon is also cursed.

At the beginning of each tablet, covering a series of acts, the Gods express satisfaction and pleasure in the preceding work; while in the Mosaic account the same satisfaction is expressed at the close of each act, or day's work. On one of the tablets is a cut or drawing, representing a tree with fruit on it, a woman on one side of it, with a serpent behind her, and a man on the other side; the woman is in the act of plucking the fruit with an outstretched hand.

Mosaic Legends of Creation

As the Mosaic account is accessible to all, we here give only its substance.

In the beginning, God created the heavens and earth, which were without form, and darkness was on the face of the deep. Light was then created, and divided from the darkness. The light was called day, and the darkness night. On the second day, the firmament was made and called heaven. On the third day, the waters and land were separated, the land called earth and the water sea; the earth was commanded to produce grass, herbs, and fruit, each producing its own kind. On the fourth day, God created light in the firmament, and said Let there be signs, seasons, and years. Two great lights were then made, and set in the firmament, the sun to rule the day, the moon the night. On the fifth day, the waters were commanded to produce living creatures and fowls, each to produce its kind. On the sixth day, man was made and given dominion over all creation. At the end of each day, God expressed himself satisfied with his work.

The account then goes on and says man was made out of dust, and life breathed into him. Man was then put into a garden, watered by four rivers, called Pison, Gihon, Hiddekel, and Euphrates, and forbidden to eat certain fruit. The man was called Adam, and given a wife called Eve; she was commanded to obey her husband. The account goes on to show that the forbidden fruit was eaten, in consequence of which the pair were driven from the garden, and a flaming sword placed at the gate, turned to the four points of the compass.

The terms Adam and Eve, in the Chaldean dialect, were symbolical of earth and water, the source of all life.

It will be observed that the scenes in both the Chaldean and the Mosaic accounts were placed or laid in the valley of the Euphrates.

The Chaldean Flood Legend

As the tablets containing the Chaldean account of a flood were found in an almost perfect condition, we shall be able to give a more full account of this affair than we have given of the creation.

The name of the hero of the flood is given as Izdubar. While it is said Moses got his account from Jehovah, Izdubar gets his from Hasisadra, the man who was saved in the ark. The tablets on which these legends were inscribed are characterized as the Izdubar series, by George Smith, the author of two books, entitled "Assyrian Discoveries" and "Chaldean Genesis." The Izdubar series, as found, is a copy made from a former copy; which second copy dates back at least 2,000 years before Christ, and 600 years before Moses. How old the original was ran only be a matter of conjecture.

After lying in the British Museum for years as mere curiosities, Grotefend finally found the key, and with it unlocked the storehouse, deciphered the cuneiform characters, and gave to the world a library of ancient knowledge; among which were found the legends and myths from which Ezra copied, and palmed of¥ as of Mosaic origin, the stories of the creation and the flood. Credit is due to Mr. Young for deciphering the hieroglyphics on the Egyptian monuments. The story runs that Izdubar derived his descent from the Gods; that he was a great king, and ruled at Babylon over the cities of Akkad, Erech, Calah, and Nibur in the land of Shinar.

The biblical account makes Nimrod rule over the same cities in the land of Shinar. Izdubar and Nimrod are believed by Mr. Smith and other writers on this subject to be one and the same person. Izdubar, like Nimrod, was a great hunter, for in those days it was the custom of the king to hunt wild beasts, especially the lion. Heabani, a seer, desirous of testing the king's strength, brought him a Hon, which Izdubar at once, like Samson, slew; and now the king and Heabani become great friends and hunt together. Kusu, representing the sun, was the father of Izdubar, and the Bible says that Kusu was the father of Nimrod, who was a Cushite, and that he built Nineveh, Calah, and Resen. Josephus says Nimrod caused the tower of Babel to be built. Some writers place Nimrod at the time of Abraham. Africanus and Eusebius carry him back to the flood. Sir Henry Rawlinson says that Nergal was Nimrod deified. Rev. A. H. Sayce thinks that Nimrod was the Babylonian God, Marodah; while the decipherers of the cuneiform characters say that Izdubar was none other than the Nimrod of the Bible.

The Chaldean legends go on and say, Izdubar had a dream, that he called on his friend Heabani to interpret it. The Goddess Ishtar fell in love with Izdubar, and offered him her hand and kingdom, which he rejected, at which she became enraged, and applied to her father, the God Hea, to avenge the insult. Hea espoused her cause, and sent a bull to destroy Izdubar. Izdubar and his friend Heabani slay the beast. Ishtar, in despair, descends into Hades to invoke the powers of darkness on the head of the king. In her descent she has to pass through seven ponderous iron gates; at the first she finds a guard, who refuses to allow her to pass, alleging that no one has ever passed there except through the shadow of death. Ishtar becomes enraged and threatens to break down the gate. The keeper, alarmed, consents to open the gate, but requires the Goddess to leave the jewels of her crown. She throws them at his feet and passes to the second gate, where she has the same experience, and there further disrobes herself. In this way she passes the seven gates, at each further disrobing herself. She now reaches Hades, and appears before the Prince of Darkness in all her natural loveliness. The Demons tremble at her power, and a messenger is sent from Hades to the realms of light, to implore the aid of the great God; Hea heeds the invocation, and calls Ishtar back to earth. Heabani is now killed, and Izdubar mourns his loss, abandons his kingdom, takes a ship and a pilot, and crosses the sea in search of Hasisadra, wdio, after leaving the ark, was translated (like Enoch) to the home of the great Gods. Having learned the road to the realm where dwells Hasisadra, Izdubar crosses a barren waste of sand lo an oasis, where there are trees bearing jewels. Here Izdubar meets two beautiful women named Sidura and Sabitu, with whom he wanders until he meets Urhamsi, a boatman, when the two sail through the realms of death, and there meet Ragma, who inquires after Heabani. Here Hasisadra appears and tells to Izdubar the story of the deluge.

Hasisadra's Story of the Deluge

The story being a very long one, we give only its substance, which is as follows:

Hasisadra then said that while he was on the earth the God Hea told him that the people had become so wicked that he would bring a great flood on the earth, destroy all mankind and all living things; that he, Hasisadra, should build a ship six hundred cubits long and sixty cubits in width, and into the deep launch it; Hasisadra said to Hea, the people, old and young, will deride me. Hea then said to Hasisadra, say to them that they have turned from me, go into the ship, take thy food, thy goods, thy women servants, the female slaves, and the young men; the birds of the air and animals of the field, I will furnish to you. Hasisadra then told Izdubar that he built the ship, that its circuit was fourteen measures, that he roofed and encased it, that he rode in it on the sixth time, that he examined its exterior on the seventh time, and its interior on the eighth time. Hea said, planks against the waters I place, I repaired the rents, three measures of bitumen I placed over the sides; I then collected food and all was ready. I brought into the ship all of my male and female servants, and the animals of the field. Hea then told me that he would send the flood in the night.

Hasisadra then went on and said to Izdubar: I entered the ship and closed it up, and it rained, as Hea had told me, until the flood reached the heavens, and all life was destroyed on the earth, and during the rain the Gods in heav-

45

en wept. Hasisadra then said to Izdubar, six days and nights passed, the wind, deluge, and storm overwhelmed the earth, and on the seventh day the storm in its course was calmed. The storm and all the deluge which had destroyed life on the earth was quieted and the deluge ended.

Hasisadra further said to Izdubar: Corpses of men floated on the water, and I opened the window, and the light broke over my face, and I sat down and wept; over my face flowed my tears; I saw the shore as the boundary of the sea; for twelve measures the land rose; to the country of Nizer went the ship; the fifth and sixth day the mountains of Nizer the same; on the seventh day I sent forth a dove, it found no resting-place and returned; I then sent forth a swallow, and it finding no resting-place returned; I sent forth a raven, it saw the decrease of the waters and never returned; I sent the animals forth to the four winds; I poured out libations; I built an altar on the peak of the mountain; I built a fire and sacrificed to the Gods, who gathered over its sweet savor.

Then follows a long talk between the Gods Hea and El, and a covenant not to flood the earth again. The account then goes on to say that after Hasisadra had sacrificed, the other people came out of the ship, and when they could not see Hasisadra they called aloud for him; they heard his voice in the clouds telling them to worship the Gods.

Then follows a long conversation between the Gods, Hasisadra and Izdubar, closing by Hasisadra telling Izdubar to return to his country; Izdubar then in company with Urhamsi, the boatman, returns to Erech. Finding the city destroyed he wept and commenced to rebuild it.

The Biblical Flood

The Mosaic account of the flood is much shorter than the Chaldean legend. It commences by saying that God repented he made man, and he threatened to destroy him and every living thing on earth; he told Noah to build an ark, 300 cubits long, 50 wide, and 30 high, put a window in the top, and a door in the side; that Noah should go into the ark with his sons and their wives, take a pair of all animals to save the seed, food for all, and at the end of seven days it should rain and continue to rain forty days and nights. The account says Noah did as commanded; that it did rain forty days and nights, and all living creatures were destroyed except those in the ark; that the waters lasted one hundred and fifty days, then abated, and the ark rested on Mount Ararat; that at the end of forty days Noah opened the window and sent forth a dove, which finding no place to rest, returned; at the end of seven days he sent forth another dove, which returned with an olive leaf; and at the end of seven days more he sent forth the dove, which never returned. Noah removed the top of the ark and saw the ground was dry. All left the ark and went forth to multiply and replenish the earth. Noah then built an altar and sacrificed to the God, and the Lord smelled a sweet savor, and said in his heart that he would not again curse the ground, told Noah to multiply and replenish the earth, and he covenanted not to destroy the earth again. Noah then planted a vineyard, got intoxicated on the wine, and lived three hundred and fifty years thereafter.

Comparison of the Mosaic and Chaldean Legends

It will be seen by comparison of these accounts of an allegorical or mythical flood, that they differ only in some slight detail, such as the number of persons saved, the duration of the flood, and the kinds of birds sent out. Out of the Chaldean ship went a dove, a swallow, and a raven; while out of the biblical ark went a dove on three different occasions. The threat to destroy all living things, the command to build the ark, the animals and food to go into it to save the seed, the building of the ark, going in, the deluge, the landing on a mountain, sending out the birds on three occasions, the last one not returning, the sacrifice, the smelling a sweet savor, the blessing, and the covenant not to destroy the earth again by water are the same in both accounts, and in both stories the scene is located in the valley of the Euphrates.

The place where the ark landed, in the Chaldean account, is called Nizir; while in the biblical account it is called Ararat. The word Ararat was derived from the word Urdu, meaning high land.

When we take into consideration the probability that the authors of the Hebrew Genesis depended entirely on tradition for the story that had been handed down from generation to generation by word of mouth, it is only surprising that the Mosaic account is so good a copy of the Chaldean legend.

Accounts of Creation, by Berosus and Others

These Chaldean legends, with other accounts of an historical character, were written out and translated into Greek by Berosus, a Babylonian priest, about 360 to 330 B. C, only a little less than one hundred years after Ezra et al compiled or wrote the books ascribed to Moses. Berosus had the same source of information that Ezra possessed; his story and the Chaldean legends differ about as much as does the Hebrew story from the Chaldean, and he says that this account of the creation and the flood was an allegorical description of nature. There is another legend of creation closely resembling the one related by Berosus, which came from the city of Cutha. The copy found at Nineveh, although written in Semitic, after the consolidation of the Gods Ea, Ishtar, Zamama, Aminit, Hebo, and Samas about 2350 B. C, was evidently taken from an Accadian text, which was much older than this date, as the name of the principal hero therein was Memangab, the son of the God Benani and Belili, his wife, of Accadia.

47

Zoroaster's Account of Creation

There were other peoples and nations, much older than the Hebrews, who possessed similar stories concerning the creation of the world. In the Persian sacred scriptures, supposed to have been written by Zoroaster, who lived not later than 1800 B.C., we find an account of the creation of the world, of a first man and woman, who are called Mashia and Mashiana, who were placed in a garden, or paradise, and there were in communication with Ormuzd, the sun God; that Ahriman (the evil one), in the form of a serpent, entered the garden and corrupted the pair, who were then driven out of the garden.

The Zend-Avesta also contains an account of a deluge, where a very pious man, called Yema, was commanded by Ormuzd to build an ark and place himself and family and all pure animals therein. The command being complied with, the deluge came and destroyed all life on the earth except that in the ark. The man Yema is then commanded to go forth, subdue and cultivate the earth. Yema leaves the ark, and like Noah, one of the first things he does is to get intoxicated on wine; he then builds cities, and the earth is peopled with his descendants.

The Avesta contains the further statement, that Ahriman offered the kingdom of the world to Zoroaster if he would abjure the true religion and forsake Ormuzd. The character and doings of Ahriman as pictured in the Zend-Avesta closely resemble those given of Satan in the Christian writings.

This Persian story of the creation and flood, being of later origin than the Chaldean, like the Mosaic story was undoubtedly borrowed from Chaldea.

Hindu Account of Creation

The sacred writings of the Hindus contain an account of a miraculous creation of the world by their foremost divinity, the sun. Of their doctrines concerning a trinity, we shall have more to say when we come to speak of the Christian myths.

Scandinavian Account of Creation

The Scandinavians conceived ideas concerning the creation of the world, somewhat resembling those of the Chaldees and Hebrews. According to their theory, before the earth existed all was chaos and vapor, out of the midst of which flowed great rivers; the warm breath of the spring sun melted the ice, out of which issued a great spirit called Hel, who ruled in Helheim. This great spirit created the world, divided the day from night, separated the land from the water, placed in the heavens the sun, moon and stars, and created the animals of the land and the fishes of the sea. After this the Gods looked upon their works and saw that they were incomplete without man, so they took an ash tree, out of which they made man (an improvement over a mud man). To give him a helpmate they made woman out of an alder bush. The man they called Aske, and the woman, Embla. The supreme God took to himself a wife from a giant race; they had issue, three sons, Odin, Vila, and Ve, who became associate Gods with their father. The Gods then established their abode in a paradise called Valhalla. These people believed that the world would come to an end; that in the last days there would be war among the Gods; fire would spread over the earth, the sun would sink into the ocean, and all life would cease to exist; after which the Gods would create a new heaven and earth, and people the new earth with perfect beings, where happiness will reign forever.

This was a very ancient religion, and we cite this much of it to show how closely it resembles the sacred writings and teachings of the Hebrews and Christians.

On this array of evidence, is there room to entertain a doubt, by any reasonable man or woman, that the Bible story of creation, of Adam and Eve, of paradise, and of the sin and fall of Adam, as well as the story of the flood, are but idle tales, myths, and legends borrowed from oriental nations by the authors of the Pentateuch?

If this story be false, and false it has been clearly proven to be, what becomes of the other story, that as Adam sinned and fell, so Christ must live to redeem the fallen?

If there was no Adam to fall, then there could be no use for a redeemer. According to the Christian scheme, the two are inseparably connected, the latter depending on the former; the deduction follows that as the first story is false, the second is equally false.

The Sadducees' and Pharisees' Versions of the Messiah

At the time of the alleged birth of Christ, and for a long time prior thereto, there existed two sects or classes of Jews, the Sadducees and Pharisees. Both classes, resting their opinions on prophecy, were looking for a Messiah, a second coming of Moses, a Savior, who was to be of the House of David. This Messiah was to gather together all of the Jews in a New Jerusalem, where they were to be made happy as in their patriarchal simplicity; but as to the kind of Messiah and kingdom, as prophesied, to which they were looking forward, there was a wide difference of opinion. This prophecy, like all others, was vague, indefinite, and uncertain, capable of almost any construction. The Sadducees construed it to mean a restoration of the political kingdom as it existed under the reign of David and Solomon, and they expected to return to their long-looked and wished-for patriarchal simplicity and happiness; while, on the other hand, the Pharisees asserted that the new kingdom was to be in heaven and of a spiritual nature.

Philo, who had borrowed Plato's allegorical system, enlarged and somewhat modified it, belonged to the school of Pharisees.

Philo, profiting by the Platonic school, inaugurated and established a complete system, with an ideal or allegorical Savior, had him crucified, resurrected, and in heaven, looking after the interests of his chosen people.

In this scheme of Philo an ideal church, with its priests, bishops, and presbyters, had been created, with a full code of rules, prayers, ceremonies, etc.; in short, a complete religious system in all, or nearly all, respects like that of the Christian church as it existed after the death of Christ.

This allegorical system of Philo was in full operation at the time of the alleged birth of Christ. That the Christian scheme in all its essential parts was borrowed from the ideal teachings of Philo there can hardly be a doubt, as will be shown further on. The two systems, after the fathers of the church had established theirs, so closely resembled each other that several of the Christian fathers, as well as the followers of Philo, could not see any difference, and admitted that they were one and the same.

Origen and Philo both took the same view of the matter, which they embodied in their teachings; nor did Origen hesitate to teach the allegorical character of the system. This he found himself compelled to do, so far as the more intelligent were concerned, to keep his doctrines from being treated by this class with contempt.

We will here take leave of the legends of the Hebrews and others, go into Judea, the alleged birthplace of Christ, and explore the new religion.

Christ, or Christus: Was He a Real Character, or Was He a Myth?

Christ, or Christus as he was called by a Roman historian, was born, it is claimed, in Judea, in a little obscure town called Nazareth, 753 years from the foundation of Rome.

The first question which here arises is: Was he a real person, or an ideal being placed at the base of a religion as a foundation upon which to rear the framework of a new mythology? We use this term in its proper and true sense, for all religions, as a matter of fact, are but myths. That a man by the name of Jesus Christ once existed; that he was a Jew and lived in Judea, may be true, for Jesus has been, and is to-day, a common name among the Jews. But as to the Jesus Christ of the four gospels, the evidence clearly shows him to be a myth. The claim that Christ was the son of a God is an old pagan story too silly and childish to merit consideration. That claim is to-day only made by the man who lives by repeating stale falsehoods and worn-out legends, and by a class of men, women, and young children who have not sufficient capacity to understand plain facts when clearly presented.

The question then is, did the generally credited historical Christ of Nazareth ever live? This is an open question, to be determined one way or the other according to the weight of evidence.

50

The fact that the existence of this man has been accepted by nearly one-fifth of the inhabitants of the earth, for nearly 2,000 years, would, under ordinary circumstances, raise at least a very strong presumption of the real existence of the man, thereby throwing the onus, or burden, of refuting this presumption on the party raising the issue. I say, under ordinary circumstances. The facts that the best evidence on this question has been suppressed, and that the power of the church has been used without stint to suppress investigation, take the case out of the ordinary rule, thereby throwing the burden of proof on the church party to maintain its claim. It must be remembered that it has been only within the last few years that anyone had the privilege to question the position of the church.

The only evidence that the church has to offer is the four gospels; if these gospels are forgeries, as they have been proven to be, then the church has no evidence in support of the existence of such a man. In addition to this, the church fathers were never able even to guess, within more than 130 years, the time of the man's supposed birth (Renan); nor can they tell who was his father, or even where he was born, or what became of him between the ages of twelve and thirty. If, in fact, such a man did once live, how is all of this ignorance concerning him to be accounted for? An obscure monk, near the close of the sixth century, after prodigious labor, finally guessed that the man was born about 580 years prior thereto; even this guess was not accepted by the fathers of the church until the close of the eighth century.

The question here naturally arises, If Christ were a real being and Christianity true, why did the church destroy all of the original evidence bearing on these points, and why did the church, under the penalty of death, prohibit every attempt to investigate its claims in these matters? Does not the truth everywhere invite investigation? and is it not equally true that crime and fraud fear the light of truth? Apply this rule, and ask yourself on which side the church and its priests stand.

If the whole system or scheme of Christianity was borrowed, and the names ascribed to the four gospels are forgeries, all of which we have hereinafter shown to be the fact, why the necessity of placing a genuine person at the head of these forgeries and borrowed legends?

Christ, the actual Jesus, says Octavius B. Frothingham, in his "Cradle of the Christ," is inaccessible to scientific research; his image cannot be recovered; he leaves no writings, his followers were illiterate, the mind of the age was confused; he is reported to be a Pharisee, and a native of Nazareth. The Messiahs all started out of Galilee, all found followers. Tradition goes out of its way to connect Christ with the "House of David." The moral precepts put into his mouth, including the Sermon on the Mount, says Strauss, were such as the times called for, and so they were copied from tradition.

The critics of Strauss insist that the person of Christ must have lived; that he could not have been invented. Strange position to take, says Frothingham, in view of the fact that idealization is one of the commonest feats of mankind;

that the human imagination is constantly constructing phantoms. The materials for constructing the person being given in the Hebrew Genesis, and the plastic power being provided by Hebrew enthusiasm, the result might have been predicted.

The critics of Baur insist that the New Testament and the developments of the first century could not have been created out of Rabbinical fancies. Strauss answers this by saying, "persons are not necessarily individuals; names are often used to represent multitudes and nations; such a person was not necessary to account for the existence of the religion afterward called Christianity; the personal Christ had faded away; he had disappeared from view before the gospels were written. The conclusion is that no clearly defined traces of the person of Christ remain on or beneath the surface of Christendom."

Philo, an Alexandrian Jew, a man of great learning and influence, an extensive writer, was born 20 to 10 B. C. This great sage traveled extensively over the Roman Empire; was in frequent consultation with the Emperor and statesmen of Rome, also with the learned Rabbis of Judea at the very time when, it is said, Christ did his preaching, and at the time of his alleged crucifixion; in the face of all these facts, Philo never so much as mentions such a man as Jesus Christ in any of his extensive works.

According to the gospel stories, Christ at twelve years of age confounded the wise men of Jerusalem with his superior knowledge, then was lost sight of until thirty years of age, when for two or three years he traveled over Judea, often visiting Jerusalem, and everywhere he went was surrounded by the lame, halt, blind, deaf, and other incurables, all of whom he instantly cured by a look, a word, or a touch, and he even raised the dead.

At the end of two or three years, he was, by order of the Rabbis, apprehended, given a public trial, condemned, and put to death, and at the end of three days he arose from the dead and thereafter appeared to and conversed with great numbers of people. I may here properly ask, Why did not some one or all of these people who saw him after his resurrection come forward and in some manner or form vouch for these wonderful things? That not one of them did do so is enough to stamp the gospel stories as untrue. All of these things, according to the gospel story, took place in and around Jerusalem, a city filled with Jewish priests and other learned men, including Philo, and not one of them ever heard of any of these wonderful cures or even of the existence of the man Christ.

Let us here pause and ask any intelligent man or woman whose mind is not entirely obscured by religious superstition, whether he or she can believe these things could, in fact, have taken place and not have been seen or heard of by any one of the learned men? There can be but one answer: Suppose that one-half of these wonderful things should take place to-day, in any part of the civilized world, how long would it be before every intelligent man and woman would know of, and be talking about them? While we thus present these points, we are not unmindful of the fact that no amount of evidence, however conclusive in itself, would convince the bigoted or willfully ignorant devotee of his error. He would be like the Rev. McClintock, who, in his cyclopaedia, after reviewing all of the critics and proving beyond question that Moses did not write the Pentateuch, winds up by saying, that he prefers to believe that Moses did write the books. That is, he prefers to believe what he knows to be false, rather than believe the truth when it does not accord with his preconceived opinions - and this is equally true with a majority of the devout.

The Encyclopedia Britannica admits that Philo never heard of Christ or of the Christians.

If such a man as Christ had then lived and been a man of any note, how is it possible that he could have so completely escaped the notice of Philo?

The Rev. Robert Taylor, after a most thorough research of every known document concerning the Christians of the first century, says that he cannot so much as find an allusion to such a man as Jesus Christ.

Where were the numerous Hebrew and Roman writers during this period that they never so much as heard of Christ? Could the man have lived and gained any notoriety and all of these writers not have heard of him? It seems quite impossible.

Among his biographers, the authors of the four gospels, two of them do not mention the so-called miraculous birth, and two of the four fail to notice his so-called ascension.

Two of the most important things in the man's history are thus overlooked by his biographers.

Kant and Spinoza, in speaking of this matter, say that while it may be possible, it is not probable, that the historical man Christ ever lived; that Christianity must rest its claim on an ideal being in the form of man. Plato and Philo, with a theoretical religion almost identical with Christianity, rested their scheme on an ideal man.

And now comes the Rev. McClintock, one of the most, bigoted Christians, admitting the truth when it is against Christianity only when forced to do so, and, in this case, seeing no escape from the overwhelming force of evidence, speaking through McClintock & Strong's "Cyclopaedia of Biblical, Theological, and Ecclesiastical Literature," says: "In the conflict between Christianity and reason, Puritan theology holds Christ to be the very center of the system, that all lies in the question whether such a person, historically, be necessary. Suppose philosophy could show to the conclusion of all thoughtful men, that the person of a Christ is a self-contradiction and an impossibility, there would no longer be any conflict between Christian theology and philosophy, because with the person of Christ, would be abolished the Christian theology. Christ is not, strictly speaking, a proper name, but a designation of office. Jesus Christ, or rather Jesus the Christ, is a mode of expression as, John the Baptist, or baptizer." He further says: "In the prophetic scriptures we find this appellation given to illustrate the personage who, under various designations, is so often spoken of as destined to appear in a distant age as a great deliverer. Messiah, Christ, Anointed, is, then, a term equivalent to consecrated, sacred, set apart." After saying this, he adds, "The import of this designation as given to Jesus of Nazareth may now readily be appreciated." He further says: "Christ, Messiah, Anointed, all refer to one and the same thing, meaning the revealer of divine truth, often represented by the figure of the lamb, the vine, and fish; these words have no reference to the person."

Thus we have it from the highest ecclesiastical authority that Christ is a myth, the personification of an idea, an allegorical being, a shadow, to be made by a lamb, a vine, or a fish. This accounts for the fact that the early church fathers placed the figure of a lamb, instead of a man, on the cross.

When the author wrote the above he must have had Eusebius in his mind, who said sixteen hundred years ago that Christianity was no new thing, that it was as old as Abraham. This is putting Christianity in the background by one who has by the church been properly characterized as the father of ecclesiastical history.

Athenagoras, an Athenian Christian writer, in his "Apology to the Emperor Marcus Aurelius" (176), used Hebrew scriptures without even a mention of such a man as Christ or of Christian writings.

Dr. Reich says that Hermos, one of the Christian fathers of the first century, whose writings have come down to us, nowhere alludes to such a man as Christ. This writer, Reich, in speaking of the writings of the first century names Strabo, the elder Pliny, Plutarch, Arion, Dion, Chrisostomos, Seneca, Quintius Curtius, Philo, et al, and then says, there is not to be found in the writings of any of these men as much as an allusion to such a man as Christ, or to Christianity. It will be remembered that the writings of these men cover every event and every man of the slightest importance at that time. Strabo wrote seventeen books. His twelfth book is devoted to Palestine and the Hebrew religion. The elder Pliny's writings are a complete cyclopaedia of all things human and divine. Seneca's works treat of the very things comprised in Christian ethics, and not a mention by any one of them of Christ or Christianity.

The struggle is now fully on between the numerous critics on the one side, the most of whom maintain that Christ is a myth, and the more learned theologians on the other, who are divided in opinion. The one class is with McClintock, conceding away the person of Christ as lost, but at the same time attempting to save the creed or religion; while the other class, like the former, seeing that the four gospels have been proven forgeries, are attempting to sustain the personal existence of Christ by appealing to pagan writers. They assert that Josephus, Suetonius, Abgarus, Tacitus, Lucian, Pliny, and Celsus, in their writings, have recognized the existence of the personal Christ.

While this contest is waging hot among intelligent men, the priestlet, like all babies, is vigorously shaking his rattle-box in the ears of devout old women, silly girls, and heedless boys, unmindful and ignorant of the near approach of the critical cyclone that is about to destroy him and his Christian dogmas.

Let us see if any one of these seven pagan writers has in any way recognized the existence of Christ.

The statement in Josephus has long since been recognized by all critics to be a clear case of forgery, made in the time of Eusebius, and probably by him, as he was well known to be a forger of Christian writings.

Lucian, from the Euphrates, a philosopher of note, in his "Philopatres," is, by forced construction, made to speak of a trinity and a Galilean, who, he said, by way of ridicule, has ascended to the third heaven, where he is engaged in keeping records of the good and bad actions of men. This is nothing more nor less than a take-off or burlesque of the claims of the Christians, and is now regarded as a forgery, so says the Encyclopaedia Britannica.

As to Abgarus, king of Edessa, the church fathers reported that he wrote a letter to Christ to come and cure him of a malady, to which Christ wrote back that he would send a disciple; that Abgarus turned over to the church a picture of Christ, the letter and the pocket-handkerchief used by Christ while on the cross to wipe the sweat off his face. Eusebius believed this foolish story; but, like that told of Lucian, the whole affair is known to be spurious, says the Encyclopaedia Britannica.

As to Suetonius, in his life of Claudius, he makes mention of Chrestus, the leader of the Chrestians, a wellknown pernicious Jewish sect of that time.

As to Pliny, he wrote to the Emperor Trajan to be instructed how to deal with the Christians, who, he said, adhered to an extravagant superstition called Christianity; but in no way or manner does he recognize the existence of such a man as Christ.

Celsus wrote two books in the second century, against Christianity, in which he ridicules the claims of the Christians, and speaking from their own assertions and writings, calls their leader, Panthera, the son of a Roman soldier. In no manner does this writer recognize such a man as Christ.

The question here naturally suggests itself: Why did the fathers of the church commit all these forgeries, to prove by pagan writers the existence of their Christ, if he was a real person? The answer is obvious: he was a myth, and they not only knew it, but were the parties who created the myth with intent to cheat and defraud the people, that they, the priests, might keep in power.

Tacitus, on whose statement the Christians place their greatest reliance, belonged to the second century. He speaks of the Christians in the most contemptuous manner, calls them the followers of one Christus, who was put to death for a crime. How anyone can torture this into a recognition of Christ, it is difficult to see. In this statement Tacitus was only repeating, or reciting, the words of the Christians, but in no manner asserting or stating that there ever existed such a man as Christ.

The Encyclopedia Britannica, after recognizing the forgery in Josephus says: "Not a single fact about Jesus can be learned from Jewish writers except in the 'Unexpurgated Edition of the Talmud,' where some twenty references are made to Christ, in which he is called Panthera." This last authority, speaking further of Christ, says: "Our knowledge (of Christ) derived from heathen sources is much less than we could have desired and expected. The silence of contemporary Gentile and Jewish writers, which would be otherwise inexplicable, finds its explanation in the New Testament."

What a position! Compelled to rely on forged gospels and bogus Christian writings to sustain a forlorn hope.

Having exhausted its efforts to find some mention of Christ and Christianity by any one of the numerous pagan and Jewish writers of the first century, the church turned its attention to the tombs and catacombs of Italy, Greece, and Asia Minor, for some symbolic evidence of its hero and its creed. For this purpose, in 1578, Bario, Marchi, and Count de Rossi were appointed. After much time and labor these commissioners succeeded in finding as emblems the dove, the anchor, the olive, the lamb, the palm leaf, and the Greek letters A. O. (Alpha and Omega). At the time of these finds, it was believed that the emblems referred to Christ, but none of them bore dates back of the third century. Since these things were unearthed, the same emblems have been found among well-known Jewish catacombs, bearing dates prior to the alleged birth of Christ. Dr. Reich, after referring to the writings of the apostolic fathers, the absence of any mention of Christ by Hebrew and pagan writers of the first century, and to the result of this search among the catacombs, says the so-called evidence of Christ and Christianity rests on faith alone, without any historical evidence whatever in its support. So it seems that naked, unsupported faith is all the Christian has to rely on as a substitute for history, science, and common sense.

The Crucified Man (if There Was One), Who Was He, When and Where Was He Born?

The Christians have been taught to believe, and as a matter of course they have believed what their priests have taught them, that the crucified being was a man or a God, depending on circumstances; that his mother's name was Mary, that while she was engaged to be married to a man by the name of Joseph (whether he had any other name the records are silent) a white dove lighted on her head and by its touch conception took place; that this dove was a symbol of the Holy Ghost.

In the apocryphal Gospel of the Birth of Mary, chapter ii to viii, we are told that both Mary and her mother were the offspring of the Holy Ghost. In chapter vii we are told that the Angel Gabriel called on Mary, "filling her chamber with a prodigious light, and in a most courteous manner saluting her, said: 'Hail Mary, hail Mary, virgin of the Lord, the Lord is with you.' But the virgin, who had before been well acquainted with the countenances of angels, and to whom such a light from heaven was no uncommon thing, was neither terrified with the vision of the angel nor astonished at the greatness of the light, but only troubled about the angel's words, meditating as to their meaning; the angel replied: 'Fear not, Mary, as though I intended anything inconsistent with your chastity in this salutation.'"

The angel here tells Mary that she is a favorite with the Lord, and, as a virgin, she is to have a son who is to be the king of kings and the Lord of Lords, and that his reign is to extend to the ends of the earth; he also adds much more fine talk. Mary takes in the situation, feels flattered, "and replies not as though she were unbelieving, but willing to know the manner of it." To this the angel says to Mary: "The Holy Ghost will overshadow you without the heats of lust;" "then Mary stretched forth her hands, lifting her eyes to heaven, said: 'Behold the handmaid of the Lord; let it be unto me according to the word.'" No comments. Chapter v. As Mary advances in years, her parents forsake her. The high priest issues an order commanding all virgins over fourteen years of age to marry; Mary objects; the priest calls a council; the council issues a summons to all marriageable men to appear, staff in hand. The summons is obeyed. Among numerous others, a man by the name of Joseph puts in an appearance. Mary is the only young lady in attendance. It is ordered (probably to avoid scandal) that Mary take a husband. Silence prevailing, a dove lights on Joseph's staff; the die is cast; Joseph must marry the girl; he objects, accuses the council of entrapping him; pleads his old age and large family of children (being a widower) and the youth of Mary; excuses being declared out of order, poor Joseph is then arid there forced into betrothment, after which Mary and Joseph separate. At the end of four months Joseph is called on to fulfil his engagement; Mary is called in; Joseph does not like the looks of things, declares he has been deceived, accuses Mary of improper conduct, and threatens to break the engagement. Knowing the facts, Mary does not insist on the marriage. At -this juncture the angel puts in an appearance, takes Joseph to one side, tells him that Mary is all right and that the heir apparent is the son of the Holy Ghost and destined to rule the nations of the earth. Joseph, being a very religious man, not quite seeing the point, and feeling somewhat flattered at the prospect of having a heavenly king for an adopted son, enters into the marriage; the ceremony being over, the bride and groom return to their separate abodes. In a very short time thereafter they meet and journey to Bethlehem, where, in a cave, attended by a midwife, Mary gives birth to the God of the Christians, who after being put into diapers, and all is well, is carried down into Egypt in the arms of his mother. The rest of the story will be told in our treatise on the apocryphal gospels.

We are also told that this child's name was Jesus Christ; that his mother and Joseph resided at Nazareth, but that in order to fulfil a prophecy he had to be born in Bethlehem. Now, as Bethlehem was a long distance from Nazareth, how did the parents, or, at least, how did Joseph and Mary, come to go there? The fathers of the church got up the story that they went there to pay taxes, and while there the child was born. The people of Judea had not been taxed, and we are told that this was the first tax, and that it was levied by

Governor Quirinus. But in making up this story the chroniclers were not acquainted with the fact that Quirinus was not governor of that province until nine years after the time finally fixed by the church as the date of their hero's birth. But what signified nine years? There was a prophecy to be fulfilled, and time cuts no figure in such a case; the end justified the means, the prophecy had to be fulfilled even if it required a thousand falsehoods to accomplish the desired end. There was another prophecy to be fulfilled, the Messiah must come of the House of David, that is, he must be a lineal descendant of King David, and at the same time the Messiah is to be the son of Jehovah. This mixed affair presented a complicated problem, but the church fathers were equal to the task, as one will learn by studying the proceedings of the ecclesiastical councils.

Thus far we have assumed that the crucified man was the son of Joseph, but we must remember that this point is in dispute; probably he was filius nullius.

In the first edition of the Talmud, the hero of the Christians is referred to about twenty times, and each time he is called the son of Panthera (Encyclopedia Britannica).

Celsus, the Roman historian, in his comments on Christianity, says that Mary was divorced from Joseph, and while wandering about Judea fell in love with a Roman soldier named Panthera, who became the father of (Christ. But of this we shall have more to say hereafter. When the crucified man (if there was one) was born, and when he died, has never been ascertained. The fathers of the church tried for six hundred years to find out, and then arbitrarily fixed the date of his birth.

Let us consult the authorities as to Christ's pedigree. Julius Africanus says his friends, the church fathers, fixed it up to suit their purposes, and arbitrarily connected him with the House of David. Yes, and how did they do it? They ran the pedigree both ways, but failed to make the ends meet.

According to the first chapter of Matthew it took only twenty-eight generations to run from David down through Joseph to Christ, while according to third Luke, it required forty-three generations to run from Christ through Joseph up to David, and in the two genealogies the ancestral names were entirely different.

This discrepancy can be accounted for only on the ground that the two authors, in fabricating their stories, did not compare notes in chasing the myth, or on the hypothesis that less time is consumed in running down stream than in pulling up against the current.

The Time When the Hero was Born Being Unknown, It Was Arbitrarily Fixed

The writer in Chambers' Encyclopaedia tells us that the day and month and even the year of Christ's birth, and the time of his death, were absolutely unknown to the fathers of the church; that the date of his birth now fixed, December 25th, in the year of Rome 752, cannot be traced back of the middle of the fourth century; that the reckoning of dates from his birth did not begin until the sixth century, and that the date of his death cannot be determined.

The writer in Encyclopaedia Britannica says: "It must be admitted that we cannot determine the exact year of Christ's birth; that about 4 B.C. is, by most critics, fixed as probably about the time."

Renan informs us that, among the early fathers and others of the church who had made this matter a special study, there were one hundred and thirty-two different opinions as to even the year in which Christ was born.

John F. Blake, in his "History of the Heavens," says: "The early Christians being indifferent as to the time of the birth of Christ, it remained for a monk by the name of Denys, or Dionysius Exiguus, to fix the date of his birth. This monk lived in obscurity at Rome about 580 A. C. (Anno Christi); his nativity being unknown, he was called a Scythian, an appellation applied by the Romans to the barbarians of the extreme north."

This obscure monk was the first who made the attempt by chronological calculations to discover the year of the birth of Christ. The era fixed by Dionysius was not adopted until the close of the eighth century, when the Venerable Bede induced the church to accept it; but the church has since repudiated this adoption. The time when the year was tq commence was not agreed upon until a later date; even the date as we now have it was not agreed to without a struggle, for several of the bishops boldly asserted that there was no evidence whatever as to the time of the birth or death of Christ, and to fix a date in the absence of some evidence was to arbitrarily make a date for the benefit of the church.

When these controversies were at white heat as to Christ's birth, the three Christian sects, known as Docetes, Marcionites, and Marchacans, boldly denied the gospel story of the conception, birth, and the thirty years of Christ's life, and asserted that he first appeared, fully matured, on the banks of the Jordan, created by omnipotence (Gibbon); and, as to Mary, Christ's alleged mother, Rev. H. H. Milman, in his notes to Gibbon, asserts that the Christians of the first four centuries were ignorant of the time of the birth and death of Mary, and that the tradition of Ephesus, of her death and burial, was affirmed by decree of council. Why did not this reverend gentleman tell us the whole truth, and say that the decree was obtained by fraud, instead of suppressing this important fact? Apply the maxim, "Suppressio veri suggestio falsi." The answer, in line with his profession, is not to tell the truth when it hurts the church. Gibbon comes to the rescue, and tells us that Memnon, bishop of Ephesus, by the purchase of thirty or forty episcopal votes and by clamor and force at the council of Ephesus, procured a decree sustaining this tradition.

Had Christ any Education?

In the age when, and the country where, Christ was believed to have been born, a liberal education was only within the reach of the wealthy class of

59

people. There were no schools in the small towns, the poor had not the means nor the opportunity to acquire even the rudiments of an education, and if he, Christ, had been a man of education he would not have been the associate and companion of common, ignorant laborers, or have selected such men as apostles. These things, taken in connection with the fact that he left no writings at his death, not even so much as his signature, may in all fairness be taken as presumptive evidence that he was unable to write; and if unable to write, then we may presume that he could not read. Neither could Mohammed read or write, but this fact did not prevent him from establishing a system of religion which has spread over large portions of Asia, Africa, and Europe, and at one time nearly supplanted Christianity everywhere.

With possibly two exceptions, all the founders of religions were ignorant men, being unable to read or write.

More Messiah's than One

There were in Judea a number of persons claiming to be the Messiah, but all except Christ were suppressed before the germ had sufficiently matured to reproduce and perpetuate itself. Christ was a Jew, but who was his father is a matter of serious doubt. Celsus, as will be shown more fully hereafter, says that Christ was the son of a Roman soldier; but not a Roman historian or chronicler ever heard of the man until a century after his alleged death. Had he been a person of any note or standing, or had he said or done any unusual thing, a notice of him could not have escaped the numerous Hebrew and Roman writers of his time, nor would the church fathers have failed to learn when and where he was born and when he died. The fact that they did not know and have never been able to find out, but after centuries were compelled to arbitrarily fix dates for his birth and death, would under ordinary circumstances raise a strong presumption that he never had other than a mythical existence.

As to the foolish story of his divine parentage, there seem to have been many precedents, from some or all of which the story undoubtedly had its origin.

The story or legend concerning the birth of Plato is in all essentials the same as the one made for Christ, and from which the Christ version was probably copied; or it may have been taken from the life of Apollonius.

According to his disciples, Plato was born of a pure virgin named Perictione, who had suffered an immaculate conception at the touch of the God Apollo, and Apollo had declared to Ariston, to whom Perictione was betrothed, the parentage of the child. The Platonic legend antedates the Christian one four hundred years, and was taught and believed at the time of Christ.

The next story, closely allied to this, but much older, comes from China, where tradition says that Buddha was born of a virgin amid great miracles; that in after life he was tempted by an evil spirit called Mara, which temptation he defied.

60

Several like cases have been found. In fact, all the great pagan religions have told similar stories, some of which, in brief, are hereinafter given under other headings.

If the early fathers, in copying the Platonic legend, filled the vacuum with a myth, it was in keeping with their general conduct. Christ, if a real being, was a Jew, and preached Jewish doctrines; he did not even dream of establishing a new religion. Timid at first, after getting the aid of John he became more bold, finally conceived the idea that he was the Messiah, proclaimed himself as such and as king of the Jews.

The Jews ridiculed his claim, nor was it until after he had threatened to demolish the temple of Jerusalem that they commenced proceedings to suppress him by threatening him with prosecution. He had now carried matters too far to recant, so he boldly defied the authorities; there was nothing for them to do but arrest and try him; he knew that an arrest and trial meant death, so he braced himself up for the result.

Let us go back to the gospel story and follow him from the time when he commenced to preach in his own little town, where he soon learned to his chagrin and mortification that a prophet in his own country has no honor, for the people one and all derided him, reminded him of his mean birth and calling, and advised him to continue making plows and ox-yokes. Finding no support at home, he went to Capernaum, a little town on the shore of the Sea of Galilee, where he commenced to discourse. His mother and family followed him. The people at once ridiculed him, and when he persisted in his preaching, a mob gathered and dragged him out of town. John the Baptist was killed about this time, and the people of Galilee had taken such decided action against the new prophet that he and his disciples fled to the desert of Bethsaida, where he commenced to harangue in the small settlements. There he made a few converts among the common, ignorant people, but the hostility of the better class was so manifest against him that his mother and family deemed his life in danger. They here took a decided stand against him, excused him to the people on the ground of insanity, and insisted on his flight. So he fled and kept himself concealed for a time, and then occasionally went back to Galilee. From there he went to Tyre and Sidon, where he was threatened with violence; then he fled to parts unknown, finally sailed for Magdala, thence went to Caesarea and Philippi, where the people demanded the evidence of his Messiahship. Being unable to furnish such evidence, he took his departure for Hermon; from here he sought the most secluded retreats, after which he turned up at Jerusalem. He is banished from here, and goes back to Galilee. Finding no shelter there, he starts for Engannim. Being warned against that place, he changes his course and goes back to Jerusalem, where he is threatened with arrest. He leaves and goes to Ephraim, from there he goes back to Jerusalem, and then to Bethany. Finding no place to rest, like the bird out of the ark, and being in love with his own preaching and unable or unwilling to restrain himself, he defies all opposition and again returns to

Jerusalem, where he finds preparation for his arrest. He now goes to Mount Olives, where he secretes himself, but is finally arrested. Seeing that their martyr has not the power to protect himself, his disciples all flee, he is tried, condemned, and nailed to the cross, the same as all others condemned to death. His last words to his disciples were to take care of his mother.

This statement as to his wanderings finds its support only in the writings of his chroniclers, the truth of which lacks proper vouchers.

Had the subsequent decree of the Council of Nice, adjudging him to be one of the Gods, been in existence during these wanderings, the man might, by virtue of his own pretended power, have saved himself from these insults and final death.

The fact that in all of Christ's wanderings over Judea, the people had but one opinion concerning him (except a few ignorant followers), that opinion being that he was but an ordinary man, slightly insane on religion, would under ordinary circumstances have been sufficient evidence to settle his status.

It remained for the bishops at the council of Nice, more than three hundred years thereafter, to reverse the opinion of the people of a whole province, who tried the man while alive.

The Twenty Historical Messiahs

As we are now engaged in the discussion of the Messiah problem, it will be first in order to look over the field and see how many men have, since the advent of the alleged Christ, appeared and claimed to be the true Messiah.

Messiah, as defined in the Hebrew scriptures, is an ideal king, the king who would deliver the people of Israel from bondage. "The Christ" is nothing more than a translation of "the Messiah;" it is collective Israel, or the twelve tribes, which appear under the symbol of the son of man.

The Hebrew prophecy, as understood by the Pharisees, referred to a person; hence the great number of men claiming to be the deliverer.

We here give a list of twenty of the more prominent ones. After the time of the mythical Christ, Simon was the first of note who proclaimed himself the king and long-looked-for Messiah. He was so received by the Jews of Judea, and by them acknowledged the Messiah; he set up a government, coined money in his own name, and raised a large army to oppose the Roman Emperor. Hadrian sent an army against him; on its approach, Simon took refuge in the town of Either, where he was besieged, routed, and killed.

It is said by an able historian that the Jews lost from five to six hundred thousand men in their efforts to sustain this Messiah.

During the reign of Theodosius, 434 A.C., one Moses Cretensis claimed to be a second Moses, proclaimed himself Messiah, told the Jews of Crete to follow him, and that he would divide the waters of the sea for their safe passage from the land of bondage. They left all behind them and flocked to his stand-

62

ard in great numbers; he took them to a rugged bluff overlooking the sea, from which thousands of men, women, and children rushed headlong into the waters and were drowned, at the sight of which this Messiah fled.

In the reign of Justin, 520 A. C, another Messiah, named Dunaan, calling himself the son of Moses, succeeded in procuring a large following, collected his adherents, and with them entered a small town in Arabia Felix, where he was captured and put to death.

In 529 A.C. the Jews and Samaritans rebelled against the Emperor Justin and set up as their Messiah one Julian. The emperor sent an army, which slaughtered great numbers of Jews, took the Messiah prisoner, and put him to death.

In 721 A.C. a man by the name of Jerenus arose in Spain, proclaimed himself the true Messiah, and for a time had a great number of followers.

In 1138 a Persian Jew proclaimed himself the true Messiah, succeeded in getting around himself a vast army, and in his struggle with the government was put to death, and his followers were treated with great cruelty.

In 1157 another Messiah appeared in Cordova, and succeeded in converting most of the common people, but was condemned by the better class.

In 1167 a man by the name of David Alrui arose in the kingdom of Fez, proclaiming himself the Messiah, and succeeded in getting a large following.

In the same year an Arabian Messiah appeared and pretended to work miracles. He was arrested and brought before the king, who questioned him concerning his mission. He answered he was sent by God; the king asked for a sign; the Messiah said, "Cut off my head and see me return to life again." The king took him at his word, but life failed to return.

Shortly after this a Jew beyond the Euphrates proclaimed himself the Messiah, and drew vast multitudes of people about him. He, like the others, was put to death.

In 1174 another Messiah appeared in Persia. He, like the others, had a great following of the common, ignorant people.

In 1176 David Almaner proclaimed himself the true Messiah, in Moravia. He made himself visible and invisible at will. After securing many followers, he was arrested and put to death.

In 1199 a famous magician and a man of great learning, by the name of David El David, arose in Persia, proclaimed himself the long-looked-for Messiah, raised an army, was taken prisoner, made his escape, was retaken, and put to death. Great numbers of the followers of this Savior shared the fate of their Messiah.

In 1502 a German rabbi of Venice, named Ascher, proclaimed himself Messiah, and attained quite a following in Europe.

About this time one David Reubeni proclaimed himself Messiah in Portugal. He claimed to have come from India, with the necessary credentials from heaven; by this he gained a large support among the better class.

In 1615 another Messiah appeared in India, where he gained considerable following among the Portuguese Jews.

In 1624 a Messiah appeared in the Low Countries, declared himself of the house of David, promised to destroy Rome and the anti-Christ kingdom of Turkey.

In 1666 one Sabbathai Zeb, of Aleppo, proclaimed himself Messiah and king of the twelve tribes of Israel. As this man was the greatest of all the Messiahs, he deserves a more extensive notice. Great multitudes flocked to his standard from Arabia, and other parts of Asia, who believed him to be the king of heaven and earth, who had come to deliver the Hebrew people from sin and death. Being threatened by the Mohammedan powers he gave up his claim, joined the followers of the Prophet, was given the name of Effendi, and appointed to an office.

History informs us that this man Sabbathai Zeb founded a considerable sect, which is still in existence; that he was a Jew, and that when a child he was sent to the rabbinical school, where he rapidly learned all the sacred lore of the times. At the age of fifteen he studied the Cabala, and at the age of eighteen attained the title of sage, delivered lectures, and expounded divine law. At the age of twenty-four he revealed to his disciples that he was the Messiah, the son of David, the true redeemer. Hearing of this, the sages of Smyrna notified him that he had incurred the penalty of death by violating the sacred law, whereupon he fled to Salonica, where he again set up his claim. Being there threatened, he fled, first to Athens, and from there to the Morea. Finding no friends there, he went to Alexandria, to Cairo, and thence to Jerusalem, where he remained several years teaching the Cabala, proclaiming himself Messiah, and converting thousands of people. So numerous were his followers in most places where he preached, that business was suspended, Jews sacrificed their property, and made ready to follow their redeemer to Jerusalem, the land of promise. Even the consuls received orders to inquire into this extraordinary movement.

In 1682 a German rabbi, named Mordacia, set up a claim in Italy to the Messiahship, and, after receiving quite a following, fled to Poland to save his life.

About the middle of the eighteenth century a Polish Jew proclaimed himself the Messiah, and made thousands of converts. His influence was so great that at his death four thousand persons attended his funeral.

Thus it will be seen that ignorance and religion have ever been fellow-travelers. This number of Messiahs does not exhaust the list of the historical anointed who have appeared to fulfil prophecy — nor does it include the Messiah of the Christians, because the above list is taken from profane, or, more properly speaking, civil history, of which real men and real things only are the subjects, while sacred history, which tells us of the Christian Messiah, deals in shadows, legends, and myths.

If, as the Christians claim, their Christ was the greatest and most wonderful of all the Messiahs, why did he not find a place in profane or civil history, where we have full accounts of the lesser Saviors? What does all this mean? It certainly has a meaning, and a forcible one, too. Does it mean that the priesthood of Rome borrowed a pagan religion, and a century thereafter created out of nothing a Messianic Christ, as a rallying-point around which to gather the ignorant and superstitious multitude, to be used by the Church of Rome for its aggrandizement, power, and dominion over the peoples and nations of the earth? How well they have succeeded in this, let the history of the Dark Ages tell the tale, and count the millions of innocent men, women, and children who have been murdered by orders from the heads of the church.

Further consideration of this branch of the subject will be had when we come to examine the writings concerning Christ.

The Four Gospels and Other Christian Writings as Legends and Forgeries

The four gospels contain all the evidence the church has of the existence of Christ and of his sayings and doings, in other words, his complete biography. The church must in the future, as it has in the past, stand on these gospels for its religion and its founder; if these fail, all to the church is lost. It has ever been claimed by the church that these gospels were written during the apostolic age, and by the four men to whom they are ascribed.

While some few of the leaders of the church still insist or claim that some of the matters contained in our present gospels were reduced to writing near the close of the first century, all ecclesiastical historians of to-day admit that the gospels as we have them did not exist earlier than the first half of the fourth century; and, with a few exceptions, all deny the existence of any writings whatever concerning the Christ, his sayings or doings, during the first century. The church being driven to the wall in search of Christian writings of the first century, finally falls back on the fourteen, so called, epistles of Paul, claiming that they must have been written in the first century, it being asserted by the church that Paul was born about 10 A.C. But let it be remembered that ten of the fourteen so-called epistles of Paul have been, by the most sagacious critics of Germany and France, conceded to be spurious (forgeries).

The real facts are that we have no knowledge as to the time of the birth of Paul, and as to the date of any alleged act of his the world of to-day is in blissful ignorance. See Renan's Paul, Professor White's "Warfare of Religion and Science," Dr. Reich's "History of Civilization," the American Cyclopaedia, and other works.

It may be safely affirmed that the weight of evidence is overwhelming, that not one scratch concerning Christ, or Christianity, was written for more than a hundred years after the alleged time of his death.

65

It is on what Christ is supposed to have said in his preachings that the great church has been founded. As to what his discourses were about, and what he said, much has been written and told, but very little, or nothing whatever, is known. During the first century after his death, his disciples and followers were principally concerned in getting ready for his second coming, which was to be the end of the world and the final winding-up of all human affairs; they were too busy and too much engrossed in this all-important matter to think or care to preserve the sayings of their master, or to think of establishing a new religion. The whole effort of his disciples and followers consisted in oral preachings and declamations.

Let a dozen intelligent men listen to a discussion, and then allow even five or ten years to elapse, and no two will agree, even as to the substance of the discussion. Let one hundred years elapse and then take the statements third-dand fourth-handed, and from the most ignorant sources, and what would such evidence be worth? No court of justice would give it any weight whatever. Now this is the evidence, and the only evidence, on which the church rests and asks mankind to believe what Christ said in his one, two, or three years' preaching. The proposition is simply ridiculous. It may be that, by the merest chance, the substance of some of the sayings of the man has come down to us. If so, this is all that can in fairness be expected. Most of the persons who are supposed to be contemporaries of Christ, and who heard him talk, were men of no education, rude and uncultivated.

The Gospels as Seen by Some of the Early Fathers and Others

The gospels as they have come down to us were unknown to the early fathers, and such Christian writings as they knew were not regarded by them as other than the works of ordinary men. The doctrine of inspiration was of later origin. Dr. Reich (a Greek and Latin scholar), in his "History of Civilization," says: "In the second half of the second century, the writings were divided into two parts, known as the gospels and the Acts; that Papias, who died 176 A.C., never heard of the New Testament canon; that Justin Martyr (150) refers only to the first and third gospels; that Polycarp (150-160) speaks only of fragments of gospels, and treats them as of no special authority; that no one knew or pretended to know where they came from; that the oldest manuscripts which have come down to our time are the Codex Sinaiticus, found in a convent at Mount Sinai, and the Codex Vaticanus, at Rome, both of the fourth century."

Following in the general wake, Eichhorn says: "Giescler, De Wette, Ewald, Reville (all Christian writers) agree that the gospels were taken from tradition, and that Mark was made up principally from Matthew and Luke." To the same effect see Encyclopaedia Britannica. This last authority says: "Irenaeus had a canon of his own, in which he ignored the epistles of the Hebrews, of Jude, of James, Second Peter and Third John; that Clement had a more extended collection, including some not in the present canon; that Tertullian's canon differed from all others; Muratori had a fragmentary canon, made up about 170, containing the four gospels, the Acts, the thirteen epistles of Paul, those of John and Jude, and the Apocalypse, and that some of the so-called epistles of Paul were then charged to be forgeries; that the New Testament version used in Syria did not contain Second Peter, Second and Third John; that a canon near the end of the second century was agreed to by a few of the church Bishops; that at the Council of Nice very little judgment was exercised in settling the canon beyond the books generally established by custom, but that the canon was not finally settled until the fifth century."

Sabinus, Bishop of Heraclea, affirms that, excepting Constantine and Eusebius, this council was made up of a lot of illiterate creatures, understanding nothing, and Pappus, in his synodicon to the council, says that all of the books referred to the council for determination were put under the communion-table, when the council asked God to take out the inspired ones and put them on the table, leaving the spurious ones under the table, and that it happened accordingly.

The majority of modern critics, and they are many, after most thorough research, examination, and comparison of the books with each other, have reached the conclusion that the larger part of the writings, comprising all of the books of the New Testament, are forgeries by priests and monks, made in the interest of the church, and that the fourth gospel was written at a very late period.

It is a well-established fact that these books were unknown to the world until the latter half of the third century, that they were made up from tradition and scraps of writing, picked up here, there, and everywhere in Christendom, mixed and mingled with forgeries of every kind, and that out of this heterogeneous batch of rubbish, the early fathers of the church selected what suited them, to which they added their own wishes and opinions, and thereby created a testament of the life of Christ and a code of religion. Many of the statements in these books are clear contradictions.

It is said by as able an author as Professor Westcott, that three of the compilers of these books were in correspondence at Jerusalem long enough to compare and exchange notes.

The books first appeared in Greek, while the language in Judea, where Christ did his talking, was Aramaic.

They were translated into Saxon in 721 A.C., by Bishop Egbert.

Gibbon says the history of the actions of Christ was composed in Greek during the reign of Nero and Domitian, in the cities of Alexandria, Antioch, Rome, and Ephesus. As to this matter, see later authorities hereinafter cited and quoted from.

Gibbon, in speaking of the Council of Rimini, says that the edict seeming to cast suspicion on the Homoousion standard was obtained by fraud.

The author of the notes to Gibbon in support of the text, says: "And this wicked conduct was not the exception in this particular Council, but it was the established and universal custom. Creeds were invented and successfully established by means that would disgrace a modern political caucus. Scriptures were interpolated, authorities were forged, the venal were purchased, and the ignorant were cajoled" in the interest of the church. The pious Tillemont says: "Without Eusebius we should scarcely have any knowledge of the history of the first age of Christianity;" and with him, it must be confessed that we have very little that is reliable.

The devout Lardner, in speaking of Eusebius, says: "He had great zeal for the Christian religion," and it seems too bad for Christian writers to associate his name with Satan.

Hormesdas, bishop of Rome 544 A.C., called Eusebius a forger.

It will be remembered that Eusebius was bishop of Caesarea, and that he has been characterized (very properly) as the father of ecclesiastical history.

Christianity, to the devout, virtually hangs on the writings of this man Eusebius, whom so many of his fellow-churchmen denounce as a forger and a fraud.

Dean Milman, who censures Gibbon so severely for telling the truth about the church, expresses his regret that "the fine gold so soon became dim in the Christian church." Even the Emperor Constantine, after he had become a quasi-Christian, and after having put Eusebius in the Council of Nice, as a friend, in an address to the people of Nicomedia, accused him of deceit, fraud, and forgery as to the gospels.

In his writings, Eusebius frankly admits that falsehood is justifiable in the interest of the church. He says the writings of Philo and the gospels are one and the same, that Christianity did not take its rise with Christ, that its doctrines are but the natural outgrowth of all good men.

Even Pope Boniface IX., 1310 A.C., denounced Christianity as a fraud. He said Christ was but an ordinary man, that inspiration was a lie, that the whole Christian scheme was gotten up to control the vulgar and that all intelligent men knew this to be true.

For these, and other similar sayings, Boniface was denounced as a heretic. After death his body was taken out of the grave and tried before his successor, Pope Clement, sitting with a Council (see Draper's "Intellectual Development of Europe").

Authorship and Time of the Writings

This brings us to the question of the authorship of these books, and the time when they were written or compiled.

The general belief, especially among the Christians, is that the books were written by Matthew, Mark, Luke, and John. That Mark wrote in 44, Matthew in 44, Luke in 55, and John in 96 or 97 A.C.

A few preliminary statements will be here first in order, when we will proceed to show by the highest and most reliable authority, how and when the four gospels and other New Testament writings came into existence. As before stated, there were no Christian writings during the first century. During that time the leading advocates of Christianity busied themselves in oral declamations concerning Christ and his second coming. Whatever was said concerning the new faith was called a gospel, for this was but another word for good tidings, so the early gospels were all oral. The bishops and other apostles picked up whatever they could hear concerning the new faith, proclaimed it aloud in their churches, in the streets and highways; this they continued to do until the beginning of the second century, when, becoming tired of waiting for the second coming of their Messiah, the Scribes commenced to reduce to writing the declamations and preachings of the apostles and bishops.

During the second century the new religion was proclaimed over most parts of the Roman Empire, but, as a matter of course, the understanding by different men in different localities was very much at variance, no two seeing or talking alike. This talk or teaching, not being in perfect harmony, necessarily produced dissimilar writings or gospels; but in many respects, and as to more important matters, especially concerning the second advent, the differences were slight. At the end of the second century each church, especially the churches of the large cities, had its own gospels, and each great division of territory maintained certain gospels in common. The provinces of Asia had their gospels, known as the gospels of the East; while Europe had its general gospel, known as the Western gospel; and for Africa, Alexandria had its gospels. It is needless to say that, even between these three general gospels, as they existed before any attempt to harmonize them, there were wide differences. The three, Matthew, Mark, and Luke, running in a general groove, were by reason of their resemblance called synoptic; while the gospel of John, being of much later origin, and made to heal the strife between the Hebrew and pagan factions, necessarily stands out by itself.

Attempts were made from time to time to bring together and, as far as possible, harmonize these gospels by amendments, but complete reconciliation was found impossible without a complete destruction of all, and the reconstruction of one harmonious whole; but the spirit of strife was too fierce to permit of this, so the bishops, each conceding as little as possible and claiming all he could get, brought about the numerous Councils in which all the churches were represented. But even here strife was the rule, and harmony the exception; the contending parties resorted to all manner of intrigue, artifice, deception, and even force to accomplish their ends, bringing in bands of soldiers well armed to sustain their position. By this means some of the Councils acquired unenviable reputation. The Emperor Theodosius, in 449, called a Council to settle the gospels as to the status of Christ. The Council met at Ephesus, headed by Eutyches, who brought with him three hundred monks and a body of soldiers. As usual in such Councils, sedition reigned; the outcry of the monks, with the aid of the soldiers, settled matters, and Christ was decreed to consist of two persons. This Council received the name of the "Robber Synod," says the Encyclopaedia Britannica.

The famous Council of Nice, called by Constantine, the pagan Emperor, who sat at its head, convened 325 A. C. It was this Council that made a decree settling the gospels and other New Testament books. Notwithstanding this, the decree was resisted.

We have but meagre accounts of the proceedings of this Council, owing to the fact that the fathers of the church, by order of the emperor, destroyed the records, and then denied that any records had been kept.

If the records of this Council could have been preserved and published to the world, disclosing the villainy, fraud, and rascality of the Council, the church could not even in that age have survived the shock, and this the bishops and other leaders well knew; hence the destruction and denial.

The canon of the New Testament was again amended and ratified at the third Council of Carthage, 399 A. C, and further amended at the Council of Trent, 1545. At this Council purgatory was definitely established. During all this time there was a continuous overhauling of the books by several of the bishops, who pruned to suit their own notions.

The numerous Councils, by a majority vote, declared their bodies inspired. On the majority vote depended the question of inspiration or no inspiration.

We now proceed to support our position as to the spurious character of the four gospels and other New Testament writings.

The writer in the Encyclopaedia Britannica says the Councils have been aptly called "the battle-ground of the church." There was no established creed until the Council of Nice; prior thereto all had their own creeds. This Council made a decree settling forever the creed; but notwithstanding this, the creed was enlarged at the Council of Chalcedon, 451; and at the Council of Toledo, 589, other changes were made. In speaking of the criticisms, this writer says that an influential school of critics hold that a large proportion of the New Testament books are direct forgeries; that, in fact, every book in the New Testament, except the four great epistles of Paul, is in dispute; that up to the middle of the second century, genuine and spurious books were used indiscriminately in some of the churches; and that the Council of Laodicea, in 360, prohibited the use of certain books believed not to be genuine.

Alexandrian Codex or Bible, and Others

The oldest manuscripts that have come down to us are the Codex Sinaiticus, found in a convent on Mount Sinai, and the Codex Vaticanus, in the Vatican at Rome, both of the fourth century. Next comes the Codex Alexandrinus, which is the name given to a Greek manuscript of the Old and New Testaments now in the British Museum. It was brought from Alexandria by Cyrillus Lucaris, patriarch of Alexandria, and presented to Charles I. of England, in

1628. On the page containing a list of the books of the Old and New Testaments appears an inscription in Arabic, which states that the manuscript was written by the hand of Martyr Thecla. There also appears on this document an inscription in Latin, written by Cyrillus himself, which says that Thecla was a noble Egyptian lady who lived shortly after the Council of Nice. Most critics, basing their opinion on the style of the writing and other evidence, conclude that the manuscript was written about the middle of the fifth century, while some assert that it was written as late as the tenth century. The manuscript consists of four volumes of the Old and one of the New Testament. In the manuscript most of the Gospel of Matthew, a part of John, and a part of Chronicles are missing. The famous passage in I John v. 7, "For there are three that bear record in heaven, the Father, the Word, and the Holy Ghost, and these three are one," is now generally regarded as a forgery. It appears from Cyrillus' endorsement, that the books of the Old and New Testament, as we have them from tradition, were written by this Egyptian lady, about 1,500 years ago, and a little after the Council of Nice, and that the name of Thecla was written at the end of the book, so says the American Cyclopaedia.

The Council of Nice, it will be remembered, convened in 325, and adjourned 381 A.C.

A writer in the Penny Cyclopaedia tells us that it appears on the first page of Genesis, that the manuscript was dedicated to the patriarch of Alexandria.

It will here be seen that we have the admission of the patriarch Cyrillus, that the books of the Old and New Testament were written from tradition.

Query, where did this Egyptian lady get the materials from which to write this Bible? Did she derive her information from tradition, or from older writings? And was she the first author or compiler of the Bible? And if so, did she get her inspiration in the atmosphere of oral communications, or did she take it second-hand from other writings?

As Origen, after spending twenty-eight years of his life in picking up manuscripts, commenced to make a Bible of his own, at Caesarea in 331, and the publication of the Bible containing the New and Old Testament first appeared in the fifth century, the question naturally suggests itself, who was guilty of plagiarism? Did the Egyptian lady steal Bishop Origen's scraps from which to make her Bible? or did the compilers and publishers of the fifth century commit piracy of Thecla's Bible? Probably they were all inspired pirates. Such must be the case, for we are told that the whole Bible was written by inspired men, so this Egyptian lady must have been inspired. At all events, the book took its origin in tradition, i.e., it was handed down from one generation to another by word of mouth.

We have no evidence that any part of the New Testament was given to the world prior to this time. Baur informs us that at least three of the gospels were written in a crude form, from tradition, in the latter part of the second century; that the Gospel of John was written after that time, and that all four of the gospels were from time to time thereafter modified. This opinion of

Baur is now accepted as true by all the ecclesiastical historians of Europe, but there is no evidence that these gospels were published until they went into and formed part of the New Testament, which, as before stated, was published in the fifth century; nor have we any evidence that Origen ever published his Bible. In the absence of such evidence we must conclusively presume that the dates of these publications were the first the world ever knew of these books.

The writer in the Encyclopaedia Britannica tells us that the authors of the three synoptic gospels seem to have borrowed from each other, or that all took from a common source. That Matthew and Luke borrowed from Mark, he says, has been clearly demonstrated. He also says that an original tradition existed before the three synoptics, that some common document of Christ's sayings existed before the narratives of Matthew and Luke, that other documents or traditions existed, that there is no internal evidence to determine the dates of the gospels, that Mark in many things includes the traditions from which Matthew and Luke borrowed, that the fourth gospel seems rather to be a poem or dream than a biography, that the spirit of Hebrew poetry runs through the whole record (quoting Westcott). The writer says that the earliest account of the fourth gospel is legendary; that there seems to be a joint authorship, or it was written by an amanuensis; that the gospel is the active and manifold religious thought of Ephesus, to furnish the needed assistance to Christianity as an historical religion, again quoting Westcott.

This writer, in speaking of Marcion, the Christian reformer, who lived in the second century, established a church, and had a large following, says that he, Marcion, charged the fathers of the church with fraud and forgeries as to the gospels.

Lessing, in his treatise of the gospels, tells us that the basis of all the gospels grew out of a written collection of the oral narratives of the apostles.

By a comparison of the four gospels, says Strauss, none of them appear to be genuine; their narratives are not the account of eye-witnesses, but were taken from fragmentary notes of men who lived long after the events referred to. They collected and made notes of speeches, private and public, and of all sorts of legendary traditions, and embellished them by inventions of their own. This author further tells us that about the middle of the second century there were different versions of the gospels in a crude form, and that traces of them only are found in our present ones.

Schleiermacher maintains that the four gospels were compiled from a number of disconnected documents; and Eichhorn, in his criticisms, says they came from tradition and that the written tradition was an Aramaic gospel.

In his "Post-Apostolic Age," Schwegler says the gospels were by the theological spirit of the age corrected, offensive matters stricken out and new matter inserted, and thus the church engaged in a continual production of evangelical speeches and sayings, till at last the gospel reform attained its finality in the exclusive recognition of our synoptic gospels.

In his "Lost and Hostile Gospels," Baring-Gould says that until the settlement of the canon, every church had its own gospel and knew no others; that the first gospel of the Hebrews, in a crude form, was written in the interest of the Judaizing Christians about the middle of the second century.

In Chambers' Encyclopaedia the writer says that it seems tolerably clear that, for at least a generation after the death of Christ, no attempt was made to reduce to writing any record, however brief, of the life of Christ or of his teachings. Oral traditions took the place of writings, and from such the gospels were written; that all of the gospels were taken from earlier writings and oral tradition. Finally, the Council of Carthage, in 397, sanctioned, for the West, our present gospels, made from: First, the neutral Alexandrian text; second, the written text brought to Rome from Syria; third, a non-written pre-Syrian text called Alexandrian; that the first text underwent numerous changes up to 200 A.C., and that the third, or Syrian, text, was modified up to 350 A.C. This writer further says: "There were numerous versions of the New Testament, and parts of them were picked up all over the Roman world, all taken from tradition, and made up in the second, third, and fourth centuries. The Latin originated in Africa; its date is in the second century; this version had become so mutilated that it was revised in the third and fourth centuries. The gospels were completed about 338 A.C., and the whole New Testament soon thereafter."

We will now offer in evidence the sayings of the Rev. Mr. McClintock, as taken from McClintock and Strong's "Cyclopaedia of Biblical and Ecclesiastical Literature," published in 1883. As this comes from high church sources and from a devout Christian, it should be undisputed among the faithful. The writer, after saying that the canon of the Old Testament, in its present shape, was formed gradually, beginning with Ezra and extending down to 322 B.C., reluctantly adds: "The New Testament canon presents a remarkable analogy to the canon of the Old Testament. The beginnings of both are obscure; both grew silently, under the guidance of an inward instinct, rather than by force of external authority; both were connected with other religious literature by a series of books which claimed a partial and questionable authority; both gained definiteness in times of persecutions. All of the churches of the West joined in ratifying the canon of the New Testament; each of the churches of the greatest ability collected for itself such writings as could be proven to have been the production of inspired men. These books were neither sanctioned by individuals or councils, but by natural process." He further says: "The history of the canon may be divided into three periods. The first, extending to 170, includes the era of circulation and gradual collection of the apostolic writings. The second is closed in 303, separating the sacred from other ecclesiastical writings. The third may be defined by the third Council of Carthage, 397 A.C., in which a catalogue of the books of the scriptures was formally ratified by conciliar authority. The first is characteristically a period of tradition, the second of speculation, and the third of authority, and we may trace the features of the successive ages in the course of the history of the canon. But however all this may have been, the complete canon of the New Testament, as we now have it, was ratified by the third Council of Carthage, 397 A. C, from which time it was generally accepted by the Latin church, some of the books remaining in doubt and disputed." The Council of Trent, 1543 to 1563, reformed the canon by adding all of the doubtful books, but did not settle the dispute. The writer concluded by saying, "The writings of Ferdinand C. Baur and his followers contain valuable hints as to these books."

Yes, valuable hints! as Baur characterized the four gospels, also several of the epistles, as forgeries.

How hesitatingly and begrudgingly this Rev. McClintock is forced to admit that the Old and New Testament were taken from pagan religions, that they were of slow and gradual growth, by force of a natural, or internal instinct, and not by external (divine) authority.

Just what this author means by the words "internal instinct," in this connection, is not easy to determine. In any event, it is not by divine authority.

This reverend gentleman, continuing, says: "Although the gospel was generally propagated in Asia, Europe, and Africa, there was no meeting of Christians to discuss mooted questions until the middle of the second century; the four gospels, as one collection, were generally used and adopted before the end of the second century."

In speaking of the numerous gospels afloat all over the Roman world, this writer says that some were at once rejected, while many others, such as the Gospel or History of Joseph, of the Nativity of Mary, of the Infancy of Christ, of Nicodemus, etc., were classed as apocryphal; that in these gospels (which were rejected by the Protestants) one may find the most wonderful tales concerning the infant Christ; that the Gospel of Nicodemus, found among the records of Pontius Pilate, A.C. 380, gives a graphic and vivid picture of Christ's descent into hell to liberate the spirits of the damned. As to this more will be said further on. Among the church fathers who believed and taught the story of Christ's descent into hell with the other apocryphal gospel stories, we find the names of Ignatius, Hermos, Justin Martyr, Irenaeus, Tertullian, Clement, Origen, Cyprian, Cyril, Ambrose, Jerome, Augustine, and Chrysostom. Those men used these apocryphal gospels in their attempt to prove the personal existence of their Christ, which at that time was freely denied.

Let it be remembered that this gospel, like some of the other apocryphal writings, reveled in most glowing tales and picturesque scenes of the doings of Christ, and that, like all the other gospels, it had the same origin, rested on the same evidence, and was equally well authenticated.

The substance of all of them came from pagan sources. The one as to Christ's descent into hell was undoubtedly borrowed from the Chaldean story of the Goddess Ishtar's descent into Hades.

This writer reluctantly admits the conflict between the statement in the synoptic gospels and those of John's, where, in the three gospels, it appears

Christ's teachings were laid in Galilee, while in the fourth gospel they are laid in Judea and Jerusalem.

In his "Cradle of Christ," Frothingham says: "Christianity owes its entire wardrobe, ecclesiastical, symbolical, and dogmatical, to the religions that preceded it, differing but little from paganism."

Huxley, in speaking of the gospels, says: "In my opinion it has been demonstrated that we have no knowledge of the authorship or of the date of the composition of the gospels as they have come down to us, and that nothing better than more or less probable guessing can be arrived at on that subject."

And as to the Sermon on the Mount, on which so much stress has been laid by the Christians, in their efforts to prove the purity of their hero, the very gem in the constellation of their endeavor, it may be safely asserted that Christ never uttered the words found therein. On this question Professor Huxley says: "The Sermon on the Mount, as given in the first gospel, is in the opinion of the best critics, a mosaic-work of materials from different sources." He concludes by saying, "I do not understand that this statement is challenged."

Professor Hottzmann, speaking of this matter, says "The Sermon on the Mount, as given in the first gospel, has been copied from a composition of Hebrew writings."

Professor C. W. Shields, in his efforts to support Christianity, reluctantly admits that Matthew, Mark, and Luke tell irreconcilable stories as to the crucifixion.

The Catharists, Waldenses, and Petrobrusians, Christian sects, boldly asserted, says Renan, that the established religion was a motley system of errors and superstitions,

Mosheim, an impartial ecclesiastical historian, in speaking of the Council of Nice, says: "The disputes carried on in this and other councils show the greatest ignorance and utter confusion of ideas; the will of the council was determined by a majority vote, to secure which all manner of intrigues and impositions were resorted to, including bribery and violence, and it was deemed an act of virtue to deceive and lie in the interest of the church."

Dr. Harnack, in the second edition of his "Criticisms," says that all of the so-called utterances of Christ were borrowed.

As to the origin of the gospels, the writer in Chambers' Encyclopaedia sums up the situation as follows: That during the first generation all rested on tradition; that shortly thereafter some unknown person commenced to write a collection of discourses, parables, predictions, and aphorisms in a loose way in Aramaic. About the same time Mark arranged, in Greek, his fragmentary recollections of what he had heard Peter say; this he did not scruple to supplement with other hearsay stories. The two writers were mutually complementary, and an attempt was made to combine them. After the destruction of Jerusalem there was edited in Rome the present form of the second gospel, specially for the gentile Christians. At a later date, the third gospel was compiled, taken from or dependent on Mark and other writings and traditions. These three, being similar, have been characterized as synoptic. These gospels are not independent of each other.

Jerome, Bishop of Antioch, near the close of the second century, attempted to harmonize the four gospels. About the middle of the third century, one Ammonius, of Alexandria, taking Matthew as a basis, commenced to adjust the other three to it, from which Eusebius took the hint and gave all of them a general overhauling. The most far-reaching and conclusive evidence we have against the alleged authenticity of the four gospels and some epistles, comes from four great Christian leaders of the church, Ferdinand C. Baur, David F. Strauss, I. B. Bauer, and J. E. Renan.

Ferdinand C. Baur, the founder, president, and distinguished leader of the modern Tubingen school of theology in Germany, was born at Cronstadt, June 21, 1792; died 1860. A more profound scholar Europe never had. He was the author of numerous works, mostly of a theological character. When he published his criticisms on the four gospels, so successful was he that all Christian Germany, yes, all Christian Europe, was alarmed, says the Encyclopaedia Britannica.

It will be remembered that the corps of writers on that great work were stanch churchmen, blind to everything not in the interest of Christianity; but on such a work they found themselves forced to speak the truth when facts were too plain to be disregarded.

In speaking of the gospels and other sacred writings of the Christians, Baur says: "The Epistles to the Colossians and to the Philippians, as well as the Acts of the Apostles, are spurious, and were written by the Catholic School near the end of the second century, to heal the strife between the Jew and Gentile factions; and the four gospels owe their origin to party designs; our present gospels are not the earliest documents of the kind found by the church. Before them existed a primary cycle of evangelical traditions, known by different names, as the Gospel of the Hebrews, of St. Peter, of the Ebionites, of the Egyptians, etc. These gospels are spurious, and were written during the second century, and no list of the New Testament books was made until 360 A. C. For two and a half centuries we had no Bible; the canon as it now stands was fixed by decree by Pope Innocent I., 405." In this decree the Pope threw out the books of the quarrels, so says Schwegler, the biblical critic.

The Encyclopaedia Britannica, being driven into a corner, and after commenting on Professor Baur, grudgingly says: "The four gospels remain in a shadow, but it is certain that the synoptic gospels took their present form only by degrees, and that while they have their root in the apostolic age, they are fashioned by later influences and adapted to special wants in the early church. They are the deposits, in short, of Christian traditions handed down, first of all in an oral form, before being committed to writing in such a form as we now have them; and this is now an accepted conclusion of every historical school of theologians in England, no less than in Germany, conserva-

76

tive no less than radical, and is largely the result of the Tubingen investigations. It may have been understood before, but its historical significance was not appreciated. Baur's influence can not be overrated, his great genius and learning enabled him to read the meaning of certain features of primitive Christianity hitherto imperfectly discerned, and to point future inquirers along the true road of discovery."

Baur believed, and this is now the generally accepted opinion, that the four gospels and the other sacred books named by him were made after the middle of the second century, and after the Judaistic and Ebionistic parties had been consolidated into the Catholic Church.

As the writings are traced to the Catholic school, which did not exist until after the consolidation, they could not have been written before the middle of the second century.

The Rev. McClintock, speaking of Ferdinand C. Baur, says: "For many years he devoted his great intellect to the subversion of the fundamental doctrines of Christianity; he was the founder of the Tubingen school of theology, which further developed his views and gained him a sad notoriety by its attacks on the authenticity of the New Testament; he denied the authenticity of all Pauline Epistles, except those of the Galatians, Corinthians, and Romans." This writer further says: "The numerous works of Baur comprise a complete history of Christianity, from its inception down to the present time; and he leaves a great reputation for talent, breadth of view, and industry."

What a commentary on Christianity, that this great man, reared in the faith and devoting his life to a study of the origin and source of its doctrines, should not only repudiate the church and its theories, on the ground that they were untrue, but that his facts and arguments were so irrefragable as to convince all the ecclesiastical historians of Europe, who to-day adopt his facts and conclusions, carrying with them to all learned men the evidence of the near downfall of Christianity.

In the comments of the Rev. McClintock the whole story is told: Christianity and ignorance are one and the same. To be intelligent, and to be learned in the origin of Christianity, is to repudiate it.

David Frederick Strauss followed Baur. He was born at Ludwigsburg, Jan. 27, 1808, was a student of theology at the Tubingen School, became professor and teacher of Latin and Hebrew at Maulbronn, was a great student of, and published numerous works on, theology. In 1834 and 1835 he published his two volumes of the "Life of Jesus," which, like the gospel works of Baur, created unbounded fear among all Christians, both Catholic and Protestant.

As this work is in all our libraries, where it may be had, it is only necessary here to say that he reached the conclusion that the four gospels are but legendary romance, that the names of their purported authors are forgeries, and that after a century or more of oral tradition various compilations were written. He treats the whole Christian story as a myth, a work of mere fiction invented by the fathers of the church. As to Christ, he says that after his death there gradually grew up marvelous tales concerning him, which were the spontaneous outgrowth of fiction.

Next in order of these great scholars comes I. Bruno Bauer, born at Eisenberg, Sept. 6, 1809. Like Baur and Strauss, he was a theologian and the author of numerous works, mostly of a theological nature.

In 1835 he published a work severely criticising Strauss' "Life of Jesus," but after further investigation, changed his views, followed Baur and Strauss, and maintained that the gospels, the Acts of the Apostles, and the principal Epistles of Paul were willful forgeries, written during the second century. He became so convinced of the fraudulent origin of Christianity that he deemed it the duty of the civil powers to suppress it.

Joseph Ernest Renan, whose "History of Israel" we have hereinbefore freely referred to, was a French philologist, born at Treguier, Feb. 27, 1823, studied for the priesthood, was Professor of Hebrew in the College de France, and was by the government sent to Syria as scientist. He was the author of numerous works, among which were histories of Israel, of Paul, of the Apostles, and his "Vie de Jesu." When this last work appeared, it created about the same sensation as did the works of Baur, Strauss, and Bauer. Renan's style is very pleasant and captivating, as soft and charming as that of a woman. Many of his statements are quasi-innuendoes; he is so forcible, so convincing, and at the same time so gentle and smooth, that one never tires reading him. He holds up to view the contradictions and absurdities of the gospel writings, shows that they are not the works of their reputed authors, that they were written or compiled at a much later date, from oral tradition and from scraps picked up here and there, to which were added such matters as the interest of the church called for. In short, that most of the New Testament writings are the result of forgeries and frauds. In the most gentle way, he points out the manner in which the silly and idle tales concerning the resurrection got into circulation, and notes the ignorant class which gives credence to them.

These four men, in point of learning, more especially in ecclesiastical research, have no superiors, or even equals, in Europe. They have agreed that the four gospels (giving the life of Christ) were not written by their purported authors, that they were not written till the latter part of the second century, that they were made up of scraps and oral tradition to suit the wants of the church, and that the names of the purported authors are forgeries, consequently the gospels are myths and frauds. This conclusion they reached as to several of the other Christian sacred writings.

This verdict has been approved and accepted by all of the ecclesiastical historians of England and Germany.

This is unquestionably the death of Christianity with all ecclesiastical historians, soon to be accepted by all intelligent Christians, leaving the more ignorant to follow the priestlet and die a slower death in the agonies of despair.

It would seem that we might rest our case on this, but as we have further evidence, we will here offer it.

John Tyndall says: "We have the Canon of scriptures already arranged for us. But to sift and select these writings from the mass of spurious documents afloat at the time of their compilation, was a work of vast labor, difficulty, and responsibility. The age was rife with forgeries; even good men lent themselves to these pious frauds, believing that Christian doctrine (which of course was their (doctrine) would be thereby quickened and promoted" He further says: "There are gospels and counter-gospels, epistles and counter-epistles, some frivolous, some dull, some speculative and romantic, and others not in the Canon which were of authority almost equal to that of the Canonical books." He further says: "When arguments or proofs were needed, whether on the side of the Jewish Christians or of the Gentile Christians, a document was discovered which met the case, and on which the name of an Apostle, or of some authoritative contemporary of the Apostles, was boldly inscribed. The end being held to justify the means, there was no lack of manufactured testimony; the Christian world seethed, not only with apocryphal writings, but with hostile interpretations of writings not apocryphal. Then arose a sect of Gnostics, men who knew." Discord, strife, persecutions, banishment, and torture followed as usual. Tyndall exclaims: "With terrible jolts and oscillations, the religious life of the world has run down the ringing grooves of change; a smoother route may have been undiscoverable. At all events, it was not discovered. One may have looked with despair on the excited passions and wasted energies which, after ages of strife, are shown to be mere fatuity and foolishness. Thus the theses which shook the world during the first centuries of the Christian era, have for the most part sunk into nothingness."

Tyndall might with propriety have added that several of the forgeries were proven, but proof did not prevent a forged document from going into the Canon and thereby becoming one of the inspired writings, and that the civil arm of the government had to intervene on several occasions to prevent bloodshed.

It frequently happened that an inspired document had to be amended so as to conform to other writings. Whether the document was or was not the work of an inspired writer, depended on the majority vote of the Council. These Councils at the commencement of their proceedings having voted themselves inspired, and thereby infallible, one would naturally have supposed that all of their delegates would have been of one mind, and have voted the same way. The fact that such was not the case, may be accounted for on the hypothesis that infallibility and inspiration were suspended as to the minority.

It has been often asserted, and the assertion supported with considerable proof, that after settling the canonical status of the several books and writings, a final vote was taken on the aggregate, resulting in a majority of five, and that four out of the five were bribed.

What a pity that the New Testament came so near being defeated, and that its salvation rests on five votes, and that four out of the five who cast these votes should have been accused of receiving bribes for giving to the world a code of religion. As long as the number of the Gods could not, under the pagan rule borrowed by the Christians, have exceeded three, the bribe-givers and bribe-takers, under well-settled usage, ought to have been giver cabinet positions in heaven as a reward for establishing a system by which an army of priests and clergymen have been enabled to hold lucrative positions for nearly 1900 years.

The Rev. Dr. Robert Taylor, one of the ablest ecclesiastical scholars and writers of the time, in his "Diegesis,' says: "The resemblance between paganism and Christianity as taught in the first century, was so absolute as to deceive the most learned student of the two mythologies." Mosheim admits with reluctance that even in the third century the more intelligent of the Christians could not see any difference between the two. Eusebius himself, in speaking of the pagan religion, says: "Our gospels are none other in substance than the sacred text used by the school of Philo." "The early Christians so closely followed the teachings of Philo," says Mr. Taylor, "as to copy verbatim very much of his writings." This author further says: "The copying covers the selfsame doctrine, rites, ceremonies, festivals, discipline, and psalms, and also the rules as to the bishops, priests, and deacons, the observances and claims to apostolic founders; in short, everything of the slightest importance practiced by the school of Philo was followed by the leaders of the early Christians."

Let us bear in mind that Philo lived and wrote before Josephus, and at least fifty years before the first Christian writings, and when Christ, if such a person ever existed, says Dr. Taylor, was not over ten years of age. This author further says: "Here then we have in the writings of this philosopher and historian of unquestioned veracity, living and writing up an already established religious system, more than fifty years before the earliest dates that Christian historians have assigned to any Christian document whatever, a complete system of ecclesiastical polity, its bishops, its hierarchy of bishops, its subordinate clergy, the selfsame scriptures, the selfsame allegorical methods of interpreting these scriptures, the selfsame doctrines, ceremonies, festivals, discipline, psalms, epistles, and gospels, in a word, everything and every iota of Christianity." This author further says: "Philo, while partly following Plato, taught the immortality of the soul, the doctrine of the Trinity, the manifestation of a divine man who should be crucified, and the eternal rewards and punishments of a future life."

According to the Rev. Mr. Taylor, the Christians copied their entire religious system from the theoretical teachings of Plato as modified and improved by Philo. They also seem to have copied from Plato the story of the conception and birth of their Christ. Plato lived over 400 years B.C., and for a long time after his death his followers worshiped him as one of the Gods.

It was taught and believed that Plato was born of a pure virgin named Perictione, who had conceived by a touch of the God Apollo, and that Apollo had revealed to Ariston, to whom Perictione was betrothed, that Plato was his son.

The Christian story is a good copy of the above, with a change of names only. Thus the whole outfit seems to be a borrowed concern.

In speaking of the forgeries, Mr. Taylor says: "Eusebius did not hesitate to write anything which would redound to the benefit of the church, nor to suppress any truth which seemed injurious to it." Eusebius, in lamenting the unsettled condition of the creeds, says: "What was orthodox one day is heresy the next. We make creeds at one time to be destroyed a little later, and in this our zeal, we are destroying each other."

He might have added that the factions were constantly changing places with each other; that those who were hunted, banished, and tortured as heretics one day, became orthodox the next day, and in turn persecuted their opponents.

Hudibras strikes the keynote by saying:

"What makes all doctrines plain and clear?
About two-hundred pounds a year.
And that which was proved true before,
Proved false again? Two hundred more."

Le Clerc, in his "Criticisms of the Epistles," claims that he has proven beyond question that the Platonism of Philo was borrowed, and constitutes the foundation and the entire structure of Christianity.

Basnage (Histoire des Juifs) has clearly shown that the theological works of Philo were composed before or about the time of the alleged birth of Christ.

The Cross, the Trinity, and the Creed, Were of Pagan Origin

The Rev. Dr. Taylor, in speaking of the Christian sign of salvation, says: "It should never be forgotten that the sign of the cross, for ages anterior to the Augustan era, was in common use among the Gentiles, that it was the most sacred symbol of Egyptian idolatry, that it has been found on most of the Egyptian obelisks, and that it was believed to possess all the devil-expelling virtues which have since been ascribed to it by the Christians." The posts set up along the Nile, to which were attached cross beams to indicate high-water mark, became objects of worship by the ignorant Egyptians. Jupiter bore a cross with a ram's horn, and Venus a cross with a circle.

Rev. Mr. McChntock, in his Cyclopaedia, adds his sanction to the above, by asserting that: "The cross was in general use as a sign of divinity and eternal life, among several ancient nations. It was used in the Temple of Serapis, and found in the hands of Isis, Iseris, and other divinities; it was found by Laird on the sculptures of Korsbad and Nimroud, it was carved on the walls of the temples of India, and was in common use among the Britons, Gauls, Scandinavians, and Phoenicians; and the early use of the cross among the Christians was emblematic of the vine, the fish, and the lamb."

81

From the time of Constantine to near the close of the sixth century, the Christian cross bore the emblem of a lamb, which became an object of worship by the faithful until 680, when by a decree of the general Council of Constantinople, the image of a man was substituted and the further use of the sheep was prohibited.

These signs seem to indicate that there never was a real man crucified. The lamb, the vine, and the fish, according to the Rev. Mr. McClintock, were emblematic of salvation and eternal life. Such was the use to which the cross was put by nearly all the pagan nations.

When the Christians copied and adopted the pagan rules, practices, ceremonies, and religions, they also adopted the cross, and thereby designed its use to be the same as with the pagan nations.

As to the Trinity, Dupin ("Bibliotheque Ecclesiastique") says: "The word triad, or trinity, was borrowed from the pagan schools of philosophy, and introduced into the theology of the Christians of the middle of the second century, by Theophilus, Bishop of Antioch." The trinity of Plato, says the author of the notes to Gibbon, was closely followed by Philo and St. John; and the idea of the three persons forming one essence or trinity in the Platonic philosophy is precisely the same as that in the Christian theology. Among the early Christians, the Arian faction accused the orthodox party of borrowing their trinity from the Valentinians and Marcionites, so says Beausobre ("Histoire du Manicheisme").

Among the fathers of the church, a dispute arose as to the third person who should go in the make-up of the triad, a respectable minority insisting that Mary should have the place, but the matter was compromised by giving her a position at the right hand of her son, and assigning the third place to the Holy Ghost.

Mr. Taylor, in speaking of the Eclectics, who had their school at Alexandria, says: "The most indubitable testimonies prove that their philosophy was in a flourishing state at the period assigned to the birth of Christ, that the Eclectics were the same as the Therapeuts, or Essenes of Philo, and in every rational sense that can be attached to the word, they are the real authors and founders of Christianity."

The disciples of Plato, says Augustine, admitted the beginning of the Gospel of St. John as containing an exact transcript of their own principles.

Origen, one if not the most distinguished of the early Christian leaders and writers, was born 184 and died 257 A.C. He taught that Christianity and paganism were one and the same, with a common source.

The pious Lardner says of Origen: "He undoubtedly was the most distinguished, wisest, greatest, and best man that was ever engaged in promoting Christianity."

Mr. Taylor says of him that he was the first author who gave us a distinct catalogue of the New Testament: 'The sacred text owes its felicity to the criticisms and emendations of Origen, who pruned excrescences, exscinded the most glaring contradictions, inserted whole verses of his own pure ingenuity and conjecture; and diligently labored, by claiming for the whole a mystical and allegorical sense, to rescue it from the contempt of the wise, and to moderate its excitement on the minds of the vulgar." This author further says: "It is not to be denied that this wisest, greatest, and best man that ever bore the Christian name, relapsed at last into paganism, and worshiped the idols of his ancestors."

The reason why Origen renounced Christianity after a life spent in its support may be told as follows:

Celsus, one of Rome's greatest historians and most profound reasoners, during the reign of Hadrian, 117 to 138 A. C, published two books of criticisms on Christianity, in which he clearly demonstrated the absurdity of the Christian doctrines and claims. Following which, and as a matter of history, he proved, from Christian sources and church documents, that Mary procured a divorce from her husband, and while wandering about Judea, fell in love with a Roman soldier by the name of Panthera, who was the real father of Christ; that the boy, being in destitute circumstances, went down into Egypt to procure employment; that while there he fell in with Egyptian jugglers, from whom he learned the art of working pretended miracles; that on his return to Judea he set up a claim to the Messiahship, which he supported by his Egyptian system of miracle-workings, and that his alleged miracles were performed privately in out-of-the-way places, to slaves, women, and children, of the most ignorant class.

In the original Talmud the name of Christ several times appears, where he is always spoken of as the son of Panthera.

Celsus was a pagan author of the highest order, who had within his grasp all the then obtainable evidence pertaining to the church and its founder. While Celsus expressed serious doubts as to the real existence of Christ, but assuming on church authority or claims that such a man did live, he, Celsus, presented his facts from church sources so clearly, and made his arguments so forcible and conclusive, as to put the church on the defensive. Many of the most able writers came to the rescue, and among them Origen, whose attacks were conducted with his usual force and skill; but in the end, instead of converting the followers of Celsus to Christianity, he himself became convinced that Christianity was not only absurd in theory, but false in fact and founded on fraud, of which the fathers of the church were the authors.

Having been convinced of all this, Origen was too honest, too frank, and too sincere to continue an advocate of so false a system. So he renounced the faith and returned to the philosophical teachings of the old Platonic school.

The Apocryphal and Lost Gospels

From what has hereinbefore been shown we have learned about when and from what source came the writings now contained in the Bible, and we have also learned that a large majority of the so-called sacred writings were finally rejected by councils and authors and compilers of the Bible. Many of these rejected writings have entirely disappeared. Among the lost ones, we have a list, now known to us only through the works of commentators. But there is still a large list now extant, generally known as apocryphal, to each of which has been attached the name of some supposed author, a name said to be falsely ascribed — forged, these documents being characterized as pseude-pigraphous. We find sixteen Old Testament documents not in the Bible, which are now lost, and eighteen such documents, denominated apocryphal, now extant.

As to the New Testament Christian writings, we find sixty-seven lost documents which were commented upon during the first four centuries, and forty-two such writings generally characterized as apocryphal, which have come down to our time. As the names or titles of these documents seem a little odd, for the edification of the devout, we here append a few of them.

Among the lost documents we find an Epistle of Christ, some books under the name of Christ, an Epistle of Christ to Peter, also one to Paul; a Hymn of Christ, a Gospel of Eve, a Gospel of Judas Iscariot, a Gospel of Matthias, a Tradition of Matthias, a Gospel of Nazarenes, a Gospel of Paul, a Revelation of Paul, a Gospel of Perfection, a Gospel of Peter, Revelation of Peter, a Gospel of Titian, a Gospel of the Nativity of Mary, etc.

Among the extant apocryphal writings, we find letters of Abgarus to Christ and Christ's answer thereto; a Gospel of Pilate, Apprehension of Pilate, Death of Pilate, first Epistle of Pilate, the Descent of Christ into Hell, etc.

It must be remembered that the above list comprises only a few of the numerous documents which went to make up the pile of debris, or rubbish, out of which the New Testament writings were selected, and it must not be forgotten that all of these writings had the same origin, and were entitled to equal credit — all founded on tradition, i.e., idle stories afloat, handed down from mouth to mouth, each new recipient, on re-telling the story, giving his own version and rounding off the tale with such new matters as were likely to be most edifying to the listener.

A few extracts from the apocryphal gospels will now be in order, which we take from William Nones' Apocryphal New Testament.

The Gospel of Nicodemus

Opening scene: A great light appeared in hell. Simon arrives. Satan notifies the prince of hell to prepare to see Christ on the threshold, admits to the prince that he got up the accusation that brought Christ to trial and death. Then follows a quarrel between Satan and the prince of darkness over the threatened invasion of Hades by Christ. While the quarrel is in full blast, "on a sudden there is a voice as of thunder and the rushing of winds, saying, Lift up your gates, O ye prince, and be ye lift up, O everlasting gates, and the King of Glory shall come in." The prince becomes alarmed and orders Satan out to take sides with Christ. No sooner is Satan out than the prince shuts and fastens the brass gates, and orders his officers to prepare to defend their abode. The devil's saints now tremble and implore the prince to open the gates and let the King of Glory in. Here David and Isaiah come into the play and notify the imps of darkness that they had foretold all these things, that the dead and damned should live again.

Isaiah says: "Did I not in my prophecy say, O death where is thy sting, O grave where is thy victory?" Hearing this, all the saints call aloud to the prince to open the gates and save himself from being taken prisoner. The prince wants to know who it is that makes this imperious demand. David answers and says, It is the King of Glory, who has come to release the damned. David here gets into a temper and calls out, saying: 'Thou filthy and stinking prince of hell, open thy gates that the King of Glory may enter in, for he is the Lord of heaven and earth." Now the Lord appears in the form of a man and lights up the pit of darkness, walks in, and at once breaks the fetters which have so long held the descendants of Adam in prison. The officers of hell are seized with fear and call to know who this invader is, and why he has come to loosen the chains of the damned and light up the regions of darkness. "Then the King of Glory, trampling upon death, seizes the prince of hell, deprives him of all power and takes Adam with him to glory."

Here the scene changes. The prince upbraids Satan for bringing Christ to hell, and says to him that Jesus has opened hell and released all the prisoners. "O Satan, prince of the wicked, keeper of the infernal regions, all the advantage which to thou did accrue by the forbidden tree and the loss of Paradise, thou hast now lost by the wood of the cross."

While this wrangle is going on Christ says to the prince: "You shall now be subject to the dominion of Satan forever, in the room of Adam and his righteous sons, who are mine." The scene in hell here closes, when "Jesus stretches forth his hand and says. Come to me, all ye my saints, who were created in my image, who were condemned by the tree of the forbidden fruit and by the devil and death." By this he declares death to be conquered. All here join hands, Christ makes the sign of the cross on Adam, takes him by the hand, all then join hands and leave the prince of darkness the sole occupant of hell. Christ here turns Adam and his posterity over to Michael, the archangel, when they meet Enoch and Elijah and the two thieves who died with Christ.

The Gospel of the Infancy of Christ

In this gospel it appears that the mother gave birth to Christ in a cave at Bethlehem, attended by a midwife, after which she is presented with valuable gifts by great men. In turn she gives them one of the child's swaddling cloths, which cures all their infirmities. At the bidding of an angel, Joseph takes the mother and son down into Egypt, where they roam about from town to town performing wonderful cures. All afflicted persons who fondle or touch the infant are at once cured of maladies. While stopping at an inn, the mother washed and hung out to dry a swaddling cloth of the baby. A poor fellow nigh unto death and filled with devils, accidentally runs his head against the piece of linen and is at once cured, and all the devils are seen to rush out of his mouth. Wherever the triad go all of the great men and even the idols fall down and worship the babe. A girl afflicted with leprosy was instantly cured by touching one of the child's dirty linens. This child caused a plentiful supply of water to gush out of a tree. After the return of the triad to Judea, Christ in play with other children performed such wonders that he got the title of king; he made mud cattle and birds and caused them to run and eat and the birds to fly. When his father made mistakes in his work and got his doors, gates, and windows too short, the child at a touch gave them the proper length. In play, a boy ran against Christ and knocked him down: when on his feet again, he threatened the boy that when he went down he never would rise again; the boy fell down and died.

In short, Christ's whole life from the cradle is one of miracles.

Of the fourteen epistles contained in William Nones' "Apocryphal New Testament," the author says that Archbishop Wake (the translator) tells us that they contain a full and complete collection of all the genuine writings that remain to us of the most primitive apostolic fathers, that can with any certainty be depended upon. In the number he is mistaken, for we have forty-two. Assuming this to be true, we ask why they were rejected? The answer is obvious. They proved too much for the success of the church.

And why was the Gospel of Nicodemus rejected? It was one of the earliest gospels. Did it, too, prove too much? Was it rejected because it was not in the interest of the church to propagate the doctrine that those who died before Christ and the church existed were saved? This reason, to say the least, is plausible and in full accord with the acts of the church. After this gospel had been used and believed in by the church until the close of the fourth century, it ought to have found a place in the Canon. It is so full of dramatic life, its scenes are so delightfully portrayed, it would have afforded such a field for the display of pent mythological energy and eloquence, as well as supremely edifying to the devout listener. What a clapping of hands would have followed the portrayal of Christ's taking Adam by the hand and leading him out of hell, followed by the countless millions of liberated souls, joining hands in a string, like a rosario, all marching out of the realms of darkness to join the saints in eternal glory, leaving the poor devil solitary and alone until the arrival of the next crop of unbelievers.

What Do We Know of Peter and the Apostles?

Peter Simon, or Simon Peter, or Symeon are different names applied to the founder of the dynasty of the long line of popes.

Matthew, Mark, and Luke differ as to his nativity, and the accounts of his discipleship are as various.

The "Acts of Peter" have been shown by Baur, Schwegler, Overbeck, Zeller, and others to be spurious. Peter, Paul, and Simon Magus are very much mixed up, they are believed by some critics to be legendary characters. Peter and Paul are traced, in New Testament writings, to Antioch, where a quarrel takes place between them, "which is the last that is certainly known of Peter" (Encyclopaedia Britannica). "Tradition assigns Peter to a violent death." But of the time and place of his death we know nothing. Nothing more is said about him for over a hundred years, when Clement of Rome barely alludes to a Peter, claimed to be the Apostle.

Toward the close of the second century, tradition associates Paul and Peter as the founders of a church at Corinth, and takes them from there to Rome, where they found a second church.

This tradition seems to have originated with Eusebius and Irenaeus. The Muratorian Fragments of the second century refer to the martyrdom of Peter. A second and a third tradition pick up Peter and dispose of him in different ways.

One tradition finds Peter working at Antioch, at Babylon, and among the barbarians at the north of the Black sea, while the other takes him to Rome and then inextricably mixes him up in the legendary character of Simon Magus. The Jewish and gentile factions, in the second century, constructed a legend of romance making Peter the hero, and Paul, as Simon Magus, a false apostle (see Encyclopaedia Britannica).

All of the legends and historical romance concerning Peter originated late in the second century, doubtless among the church fathers who borrowed their materials from the alleged writings of the apostolic fathers. As the writings of the apostolic fathers have been proven to be forgeries, as we will herein show, the legends and romance founded thereon necessarily fall to the ground, leaving us without any evidence whatever that such a man as Peter ever lived.

The Twelve Apostles

It will be remembered that the Catholic church claims that Christ selected only Peter, and that Peter selected the other Apostles.

Of the history of the Apostles, says the writer in the Encyclopaedia Britannica, "we have almost no authentic knowledge beyond what is stated in the New Testament." As all of the New Testament writings touching the Apostles have been proven to be forgeries, we are left without any knowledge whatever that any Apostles were ever appointed or that any single one of the alleged twelve ever existed. Unreliable tradition and legends come to their aid.

The Apostolic Fathers and Their Writings

"Apostolic fathers" is the name given to certain Christian writers of the earliest period of Christianity of whom it was believed, and maintained by the church, that they were contemporaries and associates of the twelve Apostles, and that their writings were of the first century-. There were five of them: Clemens Romanus, Ignatius, Polycarp, Barnabas, and Hermas.

Of Clemens Romanus, nothing whatever outside of vague tradition is known. Of his birth, life, and doings we have nought but conjecture. Eusebius, who is never reliable, claims for the episcopate of Romanus the years 93 to 101. Romanus' writings, as claimed by the church, consist of one epistle from the Roman church to the Corinthian, urging a peaceful settlement of affairs. Dionysius is the first to assign the authorship of this epistle to Romanus, and gives it date at 96 or 97 A.C. But the critics deny this authorship and pronounce the epistle a forgery of the latter half of the second century.

As to Ignatius, Eusebius, who was always ready to suppress the truth when against the church and to falsify in its favor, says, as the story goes, Ignatius suffered martyrdom 73 to 101 A.C. Origen, the most reliable of the church fathers, refers to this tradition and places Ignatius' death at 109 A.C. Jerome places Ignatius among the disciples of John. All that is really known or claimed to be known of him comes through disputed epistles. Even Eusebius, in his day, pronounced eight out of the fifteen epistles ascribed to Ignatius, forgeries. Bunsen, Baur, and numerous other critics dispute the genuineness of all of these epistles, and say they were written in the second and third centuries. The writer in Chambers' Encyclopaedia says that all of the epistles ascribed to Ignatius are now universally recognized as bare forgeries.

Of the time, place of birth, and death of Polycarp little or nothing is known. The writer in Chambers' Encyclopaedia thinks Polycarp was born about 69 and suffered martyrdom about 155 A.C., and that he was bishop of Smyrna. The only writing that can now be ascribed to Polycarp is, says the Encyclopaedia Britannica, a letter or epistle to the Philippians; and this letter the Tubingen school says is not genuine.

As to Barnabas, nothing whatever is known of him. There has come down to us a work called the epistle of Barnabas, generally ascribed to him by the early fathers. "The internal evidence is conclusive against its genuineness," says the writer in the Encyclopaedia Britannica. There is no clew to its date; some assign it to 119 and 126 A.C.

The writer in Chambers' Encyclopaedia says that the epistles of twenty-one chapters ascribed to Barnabas bear the strongest internal evidence of being an Alexandrian forgery of the second century made to strengthen the church.

As to Hermas, when and where he was born and died we have no evidence.

As to his writings, "The Pastor of Hermas," a book ascribed to him, has come down to our time and is believed to have been written about 140 to

150 A.C. The modern critics tell us that the book is fictitious in form and that tliere is no good reason for supposing that the author intended to introduce any real character into it. The name of Christ does not appear in it. Irenaeus and Clement quote the book as inspired. The writer in the Muratorian Fragments concludes that Hermas wrote the book about the middle of the second century (see Chambers' Encyclopaedia). In concluding this branch of our inquiries we would say that as our information concerning the apostolic fathers comes only from their alleged writings, which have been shown to be forgeries ('The Pastor of Hermas" excepted), we are left without any evidence that any of these men ever lived (excepting, possibly, Hermas).

Thus it seems that the church was engaged in the general occupation of forging documents to prop up and support its false claims to a pernicious system of religion during the second, third, and fourth centuries.

On the foregoing evidence the case stands thus: Christ a myth; the twelve Apostles shadows; Peter a fiction; Paul a sphinx; the apostolic fathers ideal beings; their alleged writings forgeries; the New Testament writings spurious; the church a gigantic fraud.

Is it any wonder that the church, as long as it had the power, put to death all persons who attempted to investigate its origin?

Apollonius of Tyana

Did the Christian fathers steal the biography of this man Apollonius, and attach to it a mythical head called Jesus Christ? It is so charged by respectable authority; while on the other hand, some learned Christian writers charge plagiarism on Apollonius, or on his biographer, Philostratus.

In all the writings concerning this man, including the English and American Encyclopaedias, it is conceded that Apollonius was a real man, a Cappadocian, born about 4 to 6 years B.C., a man of great learning, a sage, a teacher, and a disciple of Pythagoras, and that he traveled all over the Roman world and into China and India. By the same authority it is also admitted that one Damis became his, Apollonius', life companion, traveled with him as his amanuensis, taking notes of his master's sayings and doings, and that Philostratus, a Grecian historian, born about 180 A.C., at the request of the Emperor Septimus Severus or his wife, wrote the life of Apollonius at the beginning of the second century. And by the same authorities it is conceded that Apollonius did perform what appeared to be miracles, similar to those credited to Jesus Christ, such as healing the sick, opening the eyes of the blind, raising the dead, etc., and that he performed these things, not by any pretended divine authority, but by force of power within himself and as a philosopher. All of this has been conceded by Christian writers, and that the life of Apollonius, as written by Philostratus, runs in most respects in the same grooves and parallel with the life of Christ as given in the four gospels, and that the miracles, or seeming miracles, are substantially alike in the two cases. The dispute arises where the claim to the genuineness of the miracles comes in, and as to which of the parties was guilty of plagiarism, or, in other words, stealing the biography of the other party. This must be determined to some extent by the age or time when the four gospels and Philostratus' history were written and published to the world, for neither party can be supposed to have knowledge of the writings of the other until their publication.

We will now proceed to show that Philostratus wrote and published his biography of Apollonius in the early part of the third century, and that the four gospels were unknown for a long time thereafter. That these gospels are spurious has elsewhere been shown.

It will be first in order to show what the authorities have to say about Apollonius. The pious Cudworth charges the pagans with procuring Philostratus to write up the pretended miracles of Apollonius as a parallel to those of Christ. The Rev. Dr. Parker, of England, in 1681 frequently admitted that Apollonius was a great man, who worked apparent miracles to the surprise of the most learned of men.

The writer in Encyclopaedia Britannica says that Apollonius was a Pythagorean philosopher, born at Tyana shortly before Christ; that he traveled over Asia; that the greatest reverence was paid to him everywhere, especially by the priests; that in Greece and Rome he astonished the magistrates by curing the sick and raising the dead; that he was worshiped for centuries after death, and that his statue was placed among those of the Gods.

The writer in the "Cyclopaedia of Biblical and Ecclesiastical Literature," a devout Christian, reluctantly says of Apollonius, after calling him an impostor, that he was born at Cappadocia about 4 years B.C.; that he studied with Pythagoras, traveled all over the Roman world, went to India and China; that he obtained vast influence among the learned men; that he died, with a reputation of sanctity, in the first century; that about one and a quarter centuries after his death, 210 A.C., in the reign of Septimus Severus and at the request of the emperor's wife, Philostratus, from the notes of Damis, wrote the life of Apollonius, and thereby paved the way for the general reception of the story among the cultivated classes of Rome and Greece; that the memoirs of Apollonius are in so many points a parody on the life of Christ; and that the annunciation of his birth to his mother, the chorus of the swans which sang for joy on the occurrence, the casting out of devils, raising the dead, healing the sick, the sudden disappearance and reappearance of Apollonius, the voice which called him at death, and his claim to be a teacher, with authority to reform the world, form some of the points of similarity.

Rev. Mr. McClintock, in saying that Philostratus wrote the history of Apollonius from the notes of Damis, suppressed part of the truth, to wit, that it appears on the face of the history that the author used not only the notes of Damis, but also numerous letters written by Apollonius, which were found in the palace of Emperor Hadrian, also narratives written by Maximus, a friend ~~ ' associate of Apollonius. Philostratus not only took his authority from original writings, but wrote by request of the emperor's wife, as he was a confidant of the emperor; while the materials used in the four gospels, giving the life of Christ, were handed down by tradition for a century, and then taken third-, fourth-, and fifth-hand from unknown sources, and written by unknown authors. On this state of the case, who can doubt that the history of Apollonius is entitled to more credit than the history of Christ?

In the early part of the fourth century, 306 A.C., Hierocles, then Governor of Alexandria, wrote two books against Christianity, in which he showed that the scriptures by their own contradictions destroyed themselves, and maintained that Apollonius excelled Christ in miracles. To these criticisms Origen replied with eight books, reviewing the life of Apollonius, in which he does not question the sources or credibility of Philostratus' history, or pretend that it was taken from Christian sources.

Again, what object other than to procure a true history could the emperor or Philostratus have had? On the other side, the Christian leaders had every interest to sustain their claim, as their power and dominion depended on it. Let it be remembered that elephants do not follow in the footsteps of mice.

Now as to the two men who performed the miracles — or the things which then appeared to be miracles, for no real miracle ever was performed:

Apollonius was a learned man, a great philosopher, a teacher, and an associate of the greatest and most learned men of Rome; and it was in the presence of these great and influential men, including the magistrates, that Apollonius performed his miracles; while on the Christian side the man Christ was of mean, obscure birth, a carpenter by trade, could neither read nor write, and was the companion and associate of ignorant fishermen in the most uncultivated province of the Roman Empire. And as to his miracles, or seeming miracles, they were performed in out-of-the-way places in the presence of boys, slaves, and ignorant old women.

Philostratus wrote his history of Apollonius in the early part of the third century, 210. It has been shown that the Christian gospels, even in a crude, unfinished state, did not exist earlier than the latter half of the third century, and in all probability, according to the weight of authority, were unknown to the world until a much later date, some authors say as late as the fourth or fifth centuries. But taking the earliest date, the latter half of the third century, as the time when the gospels, or life of Christ, first appeared in an unfinished state, the history of Apollonius is fifty years older than the history of Christ, and as the earlier could not borrow or steal what did not exist, it follows as a necessary deduction that, if there was any borrowing or pirating, it was the Christians who plagiarized or stole the writings of Philostratus and applied to them a mythical head.

It will also be remembered that we have conclusively shown that the four gospels were taken from pagan legends. But whatever be the truth, the life of Christ, as given in the four gospels, might have been copied or taken in whole, or in part, from Plato, Philo, Apollonius, or Pythagoras, or from the

91

pagan religions of India, China, or Persia. The probability is, that the Christians borrowed from all of them, including some things from the Hebrews and Romans. On this point the pious Mr. McClintock says: 'The stories told by historians, of Plato, of Severus Tullius, of Pythagoras, of Alexander, of Scipio Africanus, of Apollonius, of Buddha, and of others follow closely the gospel record of Christ." By reversing the order of facts, this reverend gentleman would have the unwary reader believe that all of these great philosophers borrowed their teachings from Christ, who was not born for hundreds of years after most of them were dead. This is about as honest a statement as can be expected from a clergyman. Had he said that the teachings of Christ followed closely the records of these philosophers, the fact would at once have been understood that the Christians did the borrowing.

It is to-day generally conceded among those conversant with ecclesiastical history that the whole record of Christ, from the time of his alleged birth to the time it is said he commenced to harangue the public, at the age of about 30, is a base fabrication, devoid of even the semblance of truth; and by the same authority it is reluctantly admitted that the record of him after that time and up to the time of his alleged death, stands upon little better foundation.

If the fathers of the church were capable of forging a part of the record, and this fact has been proven, may it not with equal propriety be said that they were capable of forging the other part, and that as they had the will to forge the one, they had the will to forge the other? And this forgery has not only been proven, but accepted as a fact by all the leading theological historians of Europe, as we have hereinbefore shown.

Forged gospels and forged epistles adopted into the sacred Canon by force and bribery have been accepted as divine truth by the Christians of the world.

The very existence of such a man as Christ is said to have been, was unknown to the pagan world, and unnoticed by a single pagan writer (and there were many of them) until the beginning of the second century, when they heard of him for the first time, through a class of ignorant fanatics calling themselves Christians. Even the church writers knew nothing of such a man until the second century after his alleged death, so it is not improbable that, while the church fathers were in the business of fabricating records, the very existence of the man was one of the forgeries.

The foregoing comprise only a few of the numerous church forgeries. It is a well-known fact that the Roman church as represented by the papacy claims an unbroken line of divine authority from Christ through Peter and so down through the popes to the present time, and they have supported this claim by documentary evidence, at least since the time of Dionysius Exiguus, who, it will be remembered, was the first to fix the date of the birth of Christ. This Scythian monk collected fifty, so-called, apostolic canons, short precepts, drawn from the Bible and the writings of the early fathers, also what pur-
'ed to be the decrees of several councils of the Eastern and African

churches between the years 314 and 451. To this collection there was added, later, a second part, containing letters (decretals) of the bishops from 375 to 498, to which were further added from time to time more decretals, running back to the establishment of Christianity. To these was added another collection, of Spanish origin, beginning about the seventh century, known as Bishop Isidore of Seville. These decretals took rank with the Bible itself, ran back to Christ, and constituted the basis of Christianity. It is now admitted by ecclesiastical historians and critics. Catholic as well as Protestant, that these documents are base forgeries. The church's excuse for these forgeries is that the occasion called for them.

The forged documents remained unquestioned, and quoted as authority, until the fifteenth century, when the forgeries were first discovered and exposed (see "Mediaeval Europe." by Ephraim Emerton, Professor of History in Harvard University).

Closely allied to the above comes a pious land forgery. At a very early date the church commenced to appropriate to itself immense areas of country in Italy, Sicily, Illyria, and Gaul, from the rental of which it received vast revenues. But as most of these lands had been obtained by fraud and force, the titles might be called in question, so Charlemagne, on demand of the church, confirmed, to that body, the titles to most of the Italian lands; the papacy founded its title on grants, purporting to come from Constantine. These grants, like the other forgeries, were believed to be genuine down to the fifteenth century, when they, too, were discovered to be clumsy forgeries, apparent on their face to have been the work of one of the church fathers, which will be seen on inspection of the forged decree in Henderson's "Historical Documents of the Middle Ages."

From what has hereinbefore been shown, it will be seen that the church fathers did not hesitate to commit forgeries as well as other crimes in the interests of the church. Forged gospels, forged decrees, forged epistles, forged land titles, stolen pagan writings, briberies, force, and other frauds, all go to make up the foundation of Christianity. What a sublime system of religion! It is no wonder that the devout are so strongly attached to this idol of purity.

On the foregoing showing, what is Christianity but an old, stale, threadbare, antiquated system of fables, legends, and myths which had ceased to serve the purpose of the ancient philosophers and mythologians, and had been by them cast off, to be picked up and made the foundation and superstructure which now overshadows a large part of our globe, and holds within its clerical grasp millions of otherwise intelligent human beings?

Let us call up Carlyle and listen to him while he says: "Without lamp or authentic finger-post, is the course of pious genius toward the eternal kingdom grown. No fixed highway more; the old spiritual highway and recognized paths to the eternal, now all torn up and flung in heaps, submerged in unutterable boiling mud. Oceans of hypocrisy and unbelievability, speedy end to superstition, a gentle one if you can contrive it, but an end. What can it profit any mortal to adopt locutions and imaginations which do not correspond to facts, which no sane mortal can deliberately adopt as true; and which the most orthodox of mortals can, after closing his mind to reason, persuade himself to guess that he believes?"

The Council of Nice

The third century had already passed without an established creed, a code of sacred laws, or even fixing the relations which Christ bore to Jehovah. Something must be done. So Constantine, the emperor, caused to be assembled at Nice three hundred and eighteen honest bishops, with himself as chairman, although at this time he was a pagan. [*] The council convened 325 A. C, and after several long adjournments finally adjourned 381 A. C. This body fixed a creed, settled by vote which of the numerous scripts gathered up from all sources, -with the traditions, should go into the sacred Canon and thereafter constitute the faith and belief of all true Christians for all time to come. Before proceeding to business this body decreed itself infallible. Then commenced bickering, wrangling, and quarreling over the writings to be received or rejected, so say Socrates, Sozomen, and Rufinus. Up to this time Christ had occupied the position of a martyr and hero vibrating between heaven and earth. His status must be fixed. So this honest council, aided by Constantine, the imperial murderer, by a solemn decree assigned to him a place among the Gods. By this decree and a second decree at Constantinople, May, 338, the Trinity borrowed from Hindustan, Chaldea, and Egypt was once more reinstated, and monotheism was overthrown. In thus establishing the Trinity, the Council but followed in the footsteps of earlier peoples and nations.

Sabinus, Bishop of Heraclea, in speaking of this Council of Nice, says: "With the exception of Constantine and Eusebius, the members were a lot of illiterate creatures. They vilified and libeled each other to such an extent, says Mosheim, that the Emperor had to use force to suppress them. To cover up their infamous proceedings, all of their records were burned, by order of the Emperor. It will be remembered that while this Council fixed the status of Christ, it remained for the Council of Constantinople, May 338, to create the third God, the Holy Ghost.

Most of the celestial and terrestrial heroes among the nations of antiquity were the offspring of earthly mothers begotten by the Gods. This famous Council of Nice followed the well-established rule, leaving the mother a virgin after the birth of the hero, literally copying the precedent in the case of Plato. As to the question of three in one and one in three, the Council acted not without precedent, for we have before seen how Anu, El, and Hea became one in Elohim, and how Elohim became three in Anu, El, and Hea; and in Egypt how Horus, Ra, and Tum became Jehovah. The process is a very simple one; all that is required is a dearth of intelligence and an unlimited amount of credulity. Another precedent is found in Hindu mythology, where we learn from the Vedas that the sun, personified, became Brahma, the creator and preserver of all things, and out of him sprang or issued Vishnu, afterward worshiped as Krishna. Then came Siva, a quasi-ghost, who also issued out of Brahma. After this Brahma entrusted the affairs of the world to Krishna, who became incarnate, took on the form of man, and in this guise descended to earth to look after the salvation of mankind; and at the final winding-up of earthly things he will return to earth to gather together his chosen people.

As to the ritual of the church, the whole outfit, even to the form of the prayers, was borrowed from pagan nations.

[*] Some devout writers, seeing that it was a disgrace for a pagan to preside over a Christian council, with more zeal than honesty, have attempted to show that he was a Christian before that event, but the most reliable authority is adverse to this contention.

What Do We Know of the Sayings and Doings of Christ?

At this point, and on the foregoing record, the question recurs: What do we know of the sayings and doings of Christ? If all the persons who have been concerned in gathering up and perpetuating his record had been honest, it would even then readily be seen that our knowledge of him, to say the least, is extremely uncertain; and when we take into consideration the interest the great army of priests and clergy have ever had to deceive the people that they might live in ease and luxury, on the credulity of the populace, and the further known fact that the priests and clergy have never scrupled at the means to accomplish their desired end, may we not in all candor assume that we know little or nothing concerning the man Christ? This is on the assumption that the man once lived.

It is said of him that he worked miracles, that he healed the sick, cured the blind, and raised the dead. As to the alleged miracles, no one of ordinary intelligence in this age believes them. The alleged flight of the parents with the child into Egypt, and his return, were copied from the Hebrew legend of the return of Moses into Egypt. The Hebrew narrative reads: "Return into Egypt, for all the men are dead which sought thy life." The legend continues: "And Moses took his wife and sons and set them upon an ass, and he returned to the land of Egypt." The language used by the evangelist is: "And take the young child and his mother and go into the land of Israel, for they are all dead which sought the young child's life."

Moses got his order from Jehovah, while Joseph got his from an angel; in both cases the parents rode on an ass. The evangelical statement, that the boy Christ "increased in wisdom and strength, and in favor with God and men," runs parallel with the Hebrew statement about Samuel, 'That he grew and was in favor both with the Lord and with men."

95

The suffering of Moses in the desert forty years, and the temptation and suffering of Christ in the desert forty days, are of the same piece. The forty days of Moses on Mount Sinai, his forty years in the wilderness, the forty days of Christ in the wilderness, and the forty days of Elijah are but mythical round numbers borrowed from the pagans. These things and the statements of the discussions of Christ, when a boy, are but idle tales invented by the early fathers of the church to bolster up their cause.

Pagan Miracles

We have said that no one of intelligence in this age believes in miracles, but if we are mistaken in this, and there are such persons, who, from the force of early teachings, should take issue with us on this point, for their benefit and edification we will cite a few among the many pagan miracles, all of earlier dates, and all parallel with the Hebrew and Christian articles.

It was said and believed that Anius, high priest of Apollo, changed stone into wheat and wine.

As Christ was begotten by the Holy Ghost, so Alexander the Great was begotten by Zeus, and so the elder Scipio was begotten by Jupiter.

The Apis bull of Egypt was born from a cow impregnated by a ray of the sun, the divine soul of Osiris having entered into it when a calf; he was carried to Heliopolis, where he was worshiped forty days. As Augustus was the son of Apollo, why should not Christ be the son of Jehovah, for it was a common thing for the Gods of those times to share the couches of married women?

Romulus and Remus, the founders of Rome, were miraculously born of the vestal virgin Ilia, with Apollo as their father; and like Christ they appeared to many persons after death.

Argus and Vulcan were born of the Goddess Juno begotten by a God. Painkhi, king of Upper Egypt, had engraved on his monument the statement that he was born of a divine egg of his mother, impregnated by the God Ra.

Aesculapius, son of Apollo, raised the dead by bringing to life Hippolitus, son of Theseus, at the request of Diana.

Hercules raised from the dead Alceste, wife of Adonetus, king of Thessalia, and restored her to her husband.

As Moses made water gush from a rock, so Minerva made oil spring from a rock.

Matthew said the star followed the Magi from the East and rested over the new-born infant at Bethlehem.

Justin says at the birth of Mithridates a comet appeared four hours a day for seventy days, so large as to fill one-fourth of the sky.

Apollonius rivaled Christ in curing the sick and raising the dead. He astonished the priests and magistrates of Rome by bringing to life the dead body of a noble woman. After his death he was assigned a place among the Gods, temples were raised to his memory, and he was worshiped for 400 years.

The Trojans received from heaven their idol Pallas.

Tros, king of Troy, was translated to heaven by Zeus.

The holy women of the temple of Diana and the priests of the Goddess Feronia walked barefooted on burning coals of fire made in honor of Apollo.

As an offset to the ram offered in sacrifice, in lieu of Isaac, the Goddess Vesta offered a heifer in sacrifice in the place of Metella.

The horse of Pegasus, by the stroke of his foot, like Moses with the tip of his staff, caused water to gush from a rock.

Pelopes, son of Tantalus, king of Phrygia, having been torn to pieces as a sacrifice to the Gods, the pieces were gathered up, joined, and life was restored.

As Jehovah revealed to the evangelists that Christ was his son, so Vulcan revealed by fire that Ceculus was his son.

Phineus, son of Mars, was born and nursed by his mother months after her death.

As the walls of Jericho fell by the sound of trumpets, so the walls of Thebes were built by the sounds of musical instruments played by Amphion.

Cyrus, the Persian king, when a child, was given up to be devoured by wild beasts, but was saved therefrom by divine interference.

D. F. Strauss, in his "Life of Jesus," says that the story of the miraculous preservation of the child Christ is but the old story told of Zeus, with a change of names only. The story told in the Pentateuch of the miraculous preservation of Moses in a basket on the Nile is but a copy of the stories told of Cyrus by Herodotus; of Romulus by Livy; of Sargon in the inscriptions; of Suetonius by Augustus, the first Roman emperor.

We might go on adding pagan miracles without number, running parallel with those told by the Jews, and of Christ by the Christians.

And we may here say that these pagan miracles come down to us just as well authenticated and supported as do those told in the Bible. They rest upon the same foundation, supported by the same class of evidence; and that foundation is a myth. The Jews and Christians undoubtedly found it easier to borrow and select from a large stock of old, stale, well-believed pagan miracles, than to invent new ones.

The Christian mythologians, being forced by the abundance of evidence to admit that all the religions of the world, like their own, claim to rest on divine revelations, finally fall back on borrowed miracles as a dernier resort to sustain a crumbling fabric.

The only genuine miracle ever performed by Christ was in selecting one man out of twelve, who could read and write. As to dreams and prophecies, the ancients had a large stock, and they were as well fulfilled as those related in the Bible.

The fine-spun but conflicting and contradictory gospel narratives of the conception, birth, and life of Christ have been by Baur, Strauss, Renan, Bauer, Greg, and others completely exploded.

The Christians will here meet us and say, even assuming that Christ was only a man, he was a wonderful teacher; he taught many valuable things. If we should concede all which has been said of him in this respect to be true, our answer will be, that all of these things had been said and taught by others long before Christ lived. The Jewish Sabbath, even the very name, was borrowed from Egypt, Chaldea, Babylon, and Assyria, as hereinbefore stated. And as to the Christian Sunday, as before shown, it was borrowed from pagan Rome.

The great Chinese philosopher Confucius taught his people to do unto others as they would be done by, nor was this any new idea originating with the Chinese. It is a natural instinct, a faculty possessed by all good men. And as for the devil, the mountain, and the kingdom story, that was borrowed from a Persian legend, where, as before stated, the devil took Zoroaster up into a mountain and offered him the kingdoms of the earth if he would forsake his religion. Substantially the same legend existed as to Buddha. Many things said to have been taught by Christ are absolutely impractical, and others, if carried out, would place us back into a state of barbarism.

The World without Christianity

The question here arises, whether the world would not be better off if Christianity had never existed? This depends on whether the church and its people have done more good than harm to the human race. The Christians and their church have left a record of their doings, and by this they must stand trial. Let us examine the record as it has come down to us.

Rome at the Time of the Origin of Christianity

At the time of the birth of Christianity, Rome was the world, and the world was Rome. Its vast empire was bounded on the west by the Atlantic Ocean, on the east by Hindustan, on the north by Germania and what now is Russia, and on the south by the great Libyan Desert of Africa; over this vast domain it held absolute dominion. To be Roman citizens was the pride of its people. Generally the people were prosperous and happy. Justice and equity were administered in all the land. There were no religious bickerings or dissensions, for all were allowed to worship the Gods, each according to the dictates of his own conscience, or to repudiate all of them. It has been said by one of the ablest historians, that if one were to select an epoch of the world's history when happiness had reached its highest point, he would elect the eighth century of Rome. Such was the state of the world at the birth of Christianity, when the ignorant worshiped all of the Gods, while the intelligent believed in none of them.

Arrogance of Christian Doctrine

The Christians from the first avowed the doctrines that their God was the only true God; that they were absolutely right, and all who did not agree with them were heretics and enemies to their creed and their God; that they were ordained by a higher power to subdue and bring into the church all mankind; and that it was their right and duty to convert the world to Christianity, and to punish those who refused to be thus converted.

The natural and inevitable result of such a doctrine, when attempted to be put into practice, was to array all others against this sect. Torture, persecution, and death to dissenters, heretics, and infidels was the natural and legitimate result of such a doctrine.

In the infancy of the church, and up to the death of Constantine, 337 A.C., the church was too weak to enforce its precepts against the pagans, and even against the heretics except by excommunication. This weapon it freely used upon those who dared to call in question the orthodox opinion; and it often happened that those who were orthodox at one time were heterodox a little later, depending on the vote of the bishops or the whim of the emperor. The church everywhere tolerated no dissenting opinions. In all ages and countries where it had the power, it enforced its decrees by torture, death, or banishment. It was only when civilization and humanity would no longer endure these outrages that the church adopted a milder form of persecution; this it did from necessity, not from choice. The church is as intolerant to-day as it was from the fourth to the seventeenth century, it has only changed its weapons and mode of warfare.

Laws of disfranchisement and ostracism are now in full force on the statute books of many of the American States. There are laws in full force and effect in several of the States depriving the unbeliever of the right to vote or hold office, and in some States he is, or was a short time ago, not even permitted to testify in the Courts.

In the State of Massachusetts, the old laws stand unrepealed, making it a penal offence, punishable by fine and imprisonment, to ride on Sunday, or for the keeper of any public-house to permit any person other than guests to stand or sit around the premises. Another law of that State, still in force, punishes with imprisonment in the State prison any person who shall deny the divinity of any one of the three Christian Gods.

In 1870 the Vatican Council at Rome issued a bull anathematizing all persons who deny that the world was made out of nothing, also all who oppose religion as promulgated by the Roman church, or who assert the doctrine of evolution, or that God and the universe are one and the same.

As late as 1875 several Catholic journals of Italy, Spain, and Belgium, joined by some priests, clamored for the restoration of the Inquisition, and asserted that without force the church was doomed.

While this was being done by the Catholics, numerous persecutions, for religious opinions, were being carried on in Protestant Sweden against men of learning for speaking disrespectfully of Christianity. In two cases, the men, for publishing Strauss's "Life of Christ," were heavily fined, and served long terms of imprisonment.

A little earlier, in 1765, at Abbeville, France, La Barre, on a charge of pulling down an old wooden crucifix, was condemned, and on June 5, 1766, was led to the place of execution, one hand cut off, his tongue drawn out with iron pinchers and cut off, after which his head was cut off. It was thereafter proven that the crucifix was blown down by a gale of wand.

In the face of the foregoing state of facts, will it do to say that the spirit of religious persecution is not as rife today as in former years? It lacks the power to enforce its demoniac spirit, and that is all the difference.

Low Character of the Early Christians

Tacitus, the Roman historian, who condescended to speak of the early Christians, in referring to the burning of Rome, says that Nero charged the crime on the persons commonly called Christians; that Christus, thefounder of that sect, was put to death as a criminal; that the pernicious superstition, suppressed for a time, broke out again, not only in Judea, where it originated, but in Rome, where all the horrible, disgraceful things from all quarters fell into it as into a common receptacle, where they were encouraged. Gibbon says that the early Christians were composed of the dregs of the populace, of peasants, boys, women, beggars, and slaves. Paul, the real founder of Christianity, after a life's effort spent in the cause, succeeded in converting and bringing into the fold from six hundred to a thousand of these worthies, says Renan. Without Paul, Christianity would have perished in the cradle, and Paul would not have died a criminal in chains at Rome. However much we may differ from him, his heroism has won from us a tear for his grave. Peter is also supposed to have died an unnatural death at Rome.

The Apostles

Out of the twelve original apostles alleged to have been selected by Christ, who were among his most intimate friends, eleven could neither read nor write; the twelfth was a tax-gatherer; the eleven were common laborers and fishermen. After the death of their master, they for a time secreted themselves in Jerusalem and in out-of-the-way places in Judea, until the death of Stephen, when a few of them came from their hiding-places and appeared in the byways as advocates of the cause of their fallen hero. Very little is known of them, and that little is found in the letters of Paul (which are charged to be forgeries), in the book of Acts, and in tradition. Tradition has consigned them all to violent deaths and ignominious graves. From this obscure root sprang

100

the Christian tree which has cast its blight and shadow over Europe and America.

Christianity, like many other budding myths, would undoubtedly have died in its cradle but for the impetuous Paul and the cool-headed Barnabas. Paul was a Jewish officer, and unrelenting in his persecution of the Christians, but he, like Brahma, became converted by a miracle, after which his impetuous temper made him as much of an enemy of the Jews as he had before been of the Christians.

Tertullian, the orator, called Paul the ringleader of the sect of Nazarenes.

A fanatic called Simon, of the town of Gitton in Samaria, commenced to preach primitive Mosaism, of which he pretended to have found the sacred utensils. He cured the sick, raised the dead, restored the blind, and did many other wonders by laying on of hands. Although a pagan and a conjurer, he was making many converts.

Philip, learning of Simon's success, rushed to his aid, followed by the apostles Peter and John, when all worked together and rivaled Jerusalem in the number of converts. Barnabas, one of the most enlightened of the Christians, seeing that this pagan Simon was likely to outdo the faithful in miracles, rushed to the aid of Paul, who was likely to destroy, not only himself, but his cause, by his own egotism and self-will; when the two acted together on the Christian side, turned their shafts against Simon and his miraculous powers, until they crushed him. In this way, and by this combination and trust, Simon lost and Christ won the place on the trinity.

Quarrel Over the Trinity and Incarnation

After the extinction of paganism, the Christian bishops and presbyters, early in the fifth century, turned their attention to the exploration of the nature and attributes of their founder. The disputes concerning the trinity were followed by those on the incarnation. Whether Christ was of pure divine or of human origin, or a mixture and compound of the two natures, made up the issue for determination; each side resorted to all manner of artifice, subterfuge, special pleas, invective, and ridicule to secure a verdict or majority vote at the synods; for a majority vote determined and settled for the time the question as to which party was orthodox and which heretic. The action and determination of one assembly generally failed to quiet and hush the threats of the minority, nor was it an uncommon thing for a synod to reverse the decree of a former one, and call from banishment the exiled heretics and fill their places in exile by those who were orthodox at a former trial.

These bitter wranglings brought to the surface three powerful sects who, in order to get rid of the notion that their hero was born of a woman and reared like other children, boldly denied that he was born at all, and asserted that he, fully matured, was let down from heaven into Judea, where, as a pure divinity, he taught the road to salvation. To get around the death scene, they asserted that it was a Jew resembling their hero who was crucified. This faction, being too small to maintain itself, was soon eaten up by the other two, who joined hands for that purpose, only to renew their quarrels after they had devoured their lesser enemy. Had these sects been successful, the road of the Christians would have been a short and easy one, for neither history nor tradition would have been in their way; a bold assertion of their hero on earth, and of his ascension to heaven, would have ended the controversy, and saved them the ever-recurring perplexity of explaining away the natural birth and boyhood of their Messiah, and his ignominious death.

This controversy was kept up for 250 years; the contagion spread until the Roman emperor was drawn into the vortex, when he used his position, and at times his army, to settle the dispute. When a point had to be settled by the army, of course all the soldiers were inspired. The quarrels raged so fiercely and became so desperate between these pious warriors, that they often brought an army of fighting Christians to the assemblies, as auxiliaries in case of need to assist in their divine work. Nor was it an uncommon thing to have a clash of arms, resulting in the sacrifice of thousands of lives.

It was a common practice with the pious bishops and presbyters, when they happened to be on the winning, or orthodox, side, to roast their heretical adversaries over slow fires, cut off their hands or feet, or tear out their tongues, as best suited their refined natures. Thousands upon thousands were thus tortured and put to death.

Sometimes both men and women were stripped naked and suspended in the air by ropes, with weights tied to their feet, where they hung until relieved by death or conversion to the true faith. The persecuted at one time became the persecutors a little later, depending on the vote of the Council or the side espoused by the emperor. All were Christians — persecuted and persecutors — differing only as to some minute or obscure doctrinal point about the trinity or incarnation; but as it was deemed necessary to salvation that the believer should not make a mistake, the end, however harsh or cruel, always justified the means.

After two hundred and fifty years of strife and bloodshed between these holy divines, aided by their devout votaries, the issues were finally settled or dropped by an agreement to ascribe to their founder, hero, and Savior, the name, title, character, and appellation of Homoousian or Homoiousian, leaving each of the contending parties to construe this term to suit itself. After thus settling the question, the mind of the pious devotee can rest at ease, for if his faith be ever doubted or called in question, all he has to do is to remember the password, Homoousian, and leave the angels or other door-keepers to interpret the oracle.

The Christian church of to-day rests upon the bones of from thirty to fifty millions of human beings guilty of no crime or offense (unless it be a crime not to understand, comprehend, or believe in the asserted divinity of Christ), who have been tortured and put to death in the most cruel and inhuman manner at the instigation, and by the authority and command, of priests, bishops, popes, and other pious leaders of the church, all claiming to act under and in pursuance of divine authority.

Quarrel Over Images

The bishops, presbyters, deacons, and other church rulers, not having all their time occupied in settling the divine nature of their hero, turned their attention to the question of the worship of images, which by the middle of the sixth century had become so thoroughly established as to supplant and usurp the place of the founder of the sect.

The walls of the cathedrals of the principal cities of Asia, Africa, and parts of Europe were decorated with pictures of Christ, the Virgin, the Holy Ghost, and numerous lesser divinities, all made without hands. The scandal had become so great that many of the bishops and deacons declared that the idols of pagan Rome had taken the place of their redeemer and martyr. A Council was called to take action in the premises. The seventh general synod, of 338 bishops, met at Constantinople, and by an edict abolished, pro forma, the worship of images. But the populace, preferring visible to invisible divinities, refused to give up their idols. An attempt to destroy these long-established objects of veneration resulted in a general conflict. The rulers were divided, the devout were impregnable. Anathemas, and decrees of excommunication, were hurled in vain; more potent weapons were resorted to, when thousands freely gave up their lives to the holy cause. After thirty-eight years of strife and carnage, the second orthodox Council convened at Nice, and revoked the former edict, thereby restoring to the Christians their pagan idols.

The priests assured the faithful that their images had promised protection to the cities of Asia, Syria, and Africa, wherein they were placed, from the ravages of the infidel Saracens; but notwithstanding these assurances the Mohammedans captured the cities and destroyed the Gods of the Christians.

Battle of Tours

After the Saracens had overrun a considerable part of Asia and Africa, planted the crescent in place of the cross, invaded and conquered part of Europe, Christianity hung by a single thread. Germany, Austria, Italy, Belgium, France, and Switzerland gathered and united their forces for the final struggle. The vast armies were quite evenly divided; the battle was fought near Tours, 732 A.C.; for six long days the battle raged with varying success; at the close of the sixth day the Christians were preparing for defeat; on the seventh day the carnage and slaughter went on, the Gods favoring the Saracens until Abd-el-Rahman, their commander, fell mortally wounded, leaving his followers in dismay to quarrel among themselves, while the Christians, led by Martel, remained masters of the field. Mohammedan invasions and conquest ceased for a time with this famous battle, and the followers of the cross once more felt at ease.

While the faithful will believe the story of Anastasius, that the success of the Christians was due to the use among the soldiers of three consecrated sponges, which prevented the spears of the infidels from piercing the bodies of the faithful, the unbeliever will continue to attribute the defeat of the Saracens to the death of their commander.

One would naturally think that, for saving the life of Christianity, Charles Martel, the hero of Tours, would have been assigned a place among the Gods, or at least among the saints, but it was not so to be, for to pay off his army for its pious work he found it necessary to appropriate a part of the church property. For this sacrilegious act he was by a Gallic synod consigned to eternal perdition. Several bishops, who claimed to be eye-witnesses at the opening of Martel's grave some years after his death, vouched for the truth that they smelled brimstone, saw fire issue from his grave, and a dragon come out of his body.

Had Abd-el-Rahman not fallen in that famous battle, the Koran would have been taught to-day in the schools, while Europe and America would have been proclaiming the praise of Allah, and of Mohammed as his prophet.

Quarrel Over the Sacrament

Closely allied to the foregoing, there arose a contest among the Lutherans, of the Reformed church, as to what constituted the substance of the sacrament. The contest lasted during the whole of the sixteenth century, and while it was equally bitter, often ending in fights, it was less sanguinary than that over the trinity and incarnation. The issues were fairly and fully presented as to whether the devout, in partaking of the sacrament, did so emblematically, or whether he, in eating the bread and drinking the claret, was eating the genuine flesh and drinking the genuine blood of his redeemer.

Such vital, substantial, ponderous, and all-absorbing questions as these, especially when urged with such power, vehemence, force, culture, and logic as the teachers of divinity alone can wield, must have been interesting and instructive, as well as amusing, to the outside world.

Whatever may be said as to the cannibalism of the materialistic party, it cannot be denied that its adherents had the advantage of solid food in their stomachs, even though somewhat stale, over their opponents, who contented themselves by living on air.

Constantine, First Christian Emperor

Constantine was born at Rome 272 A.C., proclaimed emperor by his army 306 A.C., and was an usurper when he was placed in the command of the army of Gaul, over soldiers most of whom were Christians. On his return from

Gaul with an army of 130,000 men, he discovered a sign of the cross in the heavens, which he interpreted to his soldiers as an omen of success. At the head of his Christian army, Constantine reared the cross and on it the motto, "By this sign ye shall conquer." He defeated Licinius at the head of 180,000 pagans, and thereby laid the foundation of his future greatness, as well as the foundation of the Christian church, of which he became the head. He caused Licinius to be murdered 324 A.C.

Some of the cardinal virtues in the life of this great Christian leader can hardly be out of place here. His wife Fausta he put to death by drowning her in a tank of boiling water; he beheaded his eldest son Crispus while he (Constantine) was presiding at the Christian Council of Nice; he murdered the husbands of his two sisters Constantia and Anastasia; he murdered his father-in-law Maximian Herculius; he murdered his nephew, twelve years of age, and some others.

Bishop Lardner, in speaking of these murders by Constantine, says: 'They seem to cast a reflection upon him." All of these murdered people were pagans. After these murders, Constantine applied to the pagan priest Sopater for consolation, and when told by this priest that he could do nothing for him, he killed the priest and then applied to the Christian bishops, who absolved him from the penalties of these crimes and gave him a free pass to paradise. (Purgatory had not then been created, nor was this wayside inn finally established by decree until the meeting of the Council of Trent in the fifteenth century, when to replenish the papal exchequer, this house was declared a stopping-place for all of the faithful who left funds or friends to purchase a ticket for the rest of the route). For this act of the bishops, Constantine abjured paganism and entered into full fellowship with the church, presided at the Councils, settled religious controversies, and declared what opinions were orthodox and what heterodox.

One of the most important acts of this royal murderer was to decree and settle the trinity. Constantine died 337 A.C.

Summary of the Origin of Christian Mythology

In the foregoing, we have, in brief, referred to only a few of the numerous leading critics and commentators consulted in making up this book. To have done more would have been foreign to the purposes of this little work. Should the reader desire to go more into the de tails of the various questions herein presented, in addition to the authorities herein cited, he will find under different headings in the several encyclopaedias, quite full lists of authors; and as to the critics on Christ, Christianity, and the gospels, he may find such as he desires in McClintock & Strong's "Cyclopaedia of Biblical, Theological, and Ecclesiastical Literature." Germany has furnished a large majority of these writers, France a few, while England and America have contributed freely to the corps. Each critic, of course, has his own style, to some extent different from all others. On a cursory reading, there may seem a lack of harmony, and, to a limited extent, conflicts between the numerous writers, but the discrepancy largely melts away on closer attention; at any rate, the main facts are always in sight. To those who have not the time or inclination to further pursue the subjects herein treated of, this summary or compendium, with the author's deductions from the numerous writers consulted, will come in place and be found useful.

We think the evidence warrants the statement that in the infancy of Christianity, honesty and ignorance were the only factors, and this may truthfully be said of all the ancient religions, thus putting Christianity, at the outset, on the same plane with all the ancient systems.

That a man called Jesus, the Christ, the Messiah, etc., once lived is quite probable. The facts to be inferred from circumstances, rather than from direct evidence, seem to warrant such a conclusion. The Christ, being attached to the name of Jesus, as an office, can have no other significance. What evidence we have points most strongly to the conclusion that he was the son of a Roman soldier named Panthera, and not the child of Joseph.

Leaving the four gospels out of consideration, on the ground that their authenticity is unknown and that they are spurious, we have no direct evidence whatever that such a man ever lived; but the fact that there grew up in Judea a class of men calling themselves Christians, the followers of a Christ or Jesus, would seem, in the absence of evidence to the contrary, to warrant the belief that a real man once lived who became the leader of a sect called Christians.

As to the historical Jesus Christ of the gospels, it has been proven beyond doubt that he is a myth, a shadow. But assuming the existence of a Jesus Christ, a resident of Judea, and taking Christian evidence for our principal guide, the Christ probably possessed a large amount of magnetism, and possibly understood something of the art of jugglery learned from the Egyptians. With the aid of this art and his own magnetism, he naturally drew around him a number of sightseers of the ignorant class, who believed him to possess supernatural powers. Such powers at that time and among that class of ignorant people, came as a matter of course from a supreme being.

His devotees in the course of time became numerous. They saw naught but the marvelous side, believed and told of wonderful cures performed by their master. In the course of time these tales extended beyond the borders of Judea, and as they were retold from one to another, they naturally increased in marvelousness until the hero became one of the Gods; once a God, he performed all that was expected, and all that had been foretold concerning the promised Messiah; in short, the Messiah had appeared. He probably died a natural death; but the foundation had been laid, and all the rest naturally followed. The story of his crucifixion and resurrection according to prediction, was applied, and the Christ was in heaven, soon to make his second appearance on earth and look after his chosen people. In such a frame of mind there was nothing too fabulous to conceive of and report about the departed Savior.

Amid the excitement and declamations concerning his second appearance, no one thought of writing anything concerning him; rude churches were built all over the Roman Empire, and daily discourses delivered therein by the more intelligent of the Christians. Every favorable report concerning the Christ was a piece of good-tidings, a gospel. A hundred years elapsed, and the Savior failed to appear; his followers believed themselves mistaken only as to time. The necessity of preserving the biography, the sayings and doings, of the Christ naturally suggested itself; the material for such a history was readily found in the numerous oral declarations afloat everywhere. Among these oral traditions the teachings of Philo, Plato, Apollonius, Zoroaster, Buddha, Confucius, and other pagan philosophers had become the leading features of the stock to be drawn upon; mixed with these were all manner of stories and legends too ridiculous to be entertained by the more enlightened of the Christians.

Writers everywhere sprang up. It is said that the second and third centuries were specially prolific in such writings. The writings at the East, in Asia, were tinctured largely with the religions of India, Persia, and China. Those of Africa, with the systems of Egypt and the Hebrews; while Europe called to her aid the religions of the Druids and Scandinavians.

The gospels everywhere differed. The church had become powerful in numbers, and the priests in influence, but there was no concert of action.

The priests, at all times mindful of their interests, saw the necessity of union; in union they could control. The priests of the East came together and met in Council; the Council commenced to gather up and sift out of the mass of writings such as suited their purposes, for the end in view was the power of the priesthood. The Councils, for they were numerous, selected mostly from the teachings of Philo and Plato, with a sprinkling from the Oriental systems; the great mass of other gospels was rejected, and a crude Testament, or Bible, made from the writings of the pagan philosophers, only substituting Christian names, dates, and places for pagan ones.

This same process was followed in Europe and Africa, resulting in an Eastern, a Southern, and a Western church, each having its own gospel reduced to a Bible. The priests, having gained the first point, now sought to concentrate in one church. The leading priests in the three divisions agreed to meet in Council. The first general Council, which convened at Nice, did little else than discuss rules and lay down a general plan to get into power and control the Christian populace.

The second great Council met at Nice 325 A.C., when the great work of consolidation took place; attempts to harmonize the gospels, each party claiming its own, resulted in the most direful conflict. Notwithstanding the Council had decreed itself infallible, there was a general overhauling of the books, each party conceding something for the general good — no, for power to the priesthood, for that was the end in view. A patched-up Bible was created, and the ecclesiastical power of the church centered in a priesthood ruled by bishops, who later on selected a president, called a pope.

In order to carry out their purposes, the civil powers needed to be added. Constantine, although a pagan, was called in, and promised the aid of the church and its fighting Christians, when he became a party to this infamous scheme. We have seen how he became a party and the head of the church.

The church, once in power, determined to perpetuate itself at all cost; no value was placed on the lives of the populace; the end justified any means, however harsh or cruel. The pagans and the Jews were still a power that might be used to crush the church; this power must be blotted out; Christianity must be the religion of the world, and its priesthood must rule all mankind; pagans and Jews alike must be brought into the church, peaceably if convenient, forcibly if necessary; torture and death became the rule. The church, to be supreme master, could tolerate no dissenters; dissenters were heretics; heretics must be put to death that the church might live. How well the church succeeded, and what means she used, we will tell in what follows.

Records of the Church in Evidence

We will now proceed and put in evidence some of the records of the church, from its earliest dates, especially from the death of Constantine, down to the present time. This we do in support of our side of the question: Would the world have been better off if the church had never been established?

First Crusade

We first offer in evidence the historical records of the first Crusade, with Peter the Hermit as the organizer of the great Christian army, commanded by several bishops of the holy church.

It will be recollected that this army was gathered from every part of Europe, numbering more than 600,000 fighting Christians; some have placed the number at over 1,000,000. This is exclusive of women and children, who in great numbers attended the army. Their aim, as you know, was to recover and wrest from the insolent Saracens Jerusalem and the holy sepulcher, where it is said the body of Christ had once been laid. The rendezvous, or encampment, from which to make a united start was fixed on the eastern side of the Bosporus, but before this point could be reached, the various divisions had to traverse their own dominions, and in some cases, the territory of their confederates.

An army of 600,000 men was gathered on the confines of Gaul and Germany, under the command of Walter the Penniless. So sure were the Crusaders that their God, or their Gods, for they then had three, would supply them with arms and provisions, that little precaution was taken to procure those things. Walter, from the time of starting in his own territory, commenced a system of foraging for supplies among his own Christian people. In this he met with much opposition, which, when he had sufficient force, he crushed without stint, putting to death all opponents, whether Christians or infidels.

In passing through Verdun, Treves, Metz, Spires, and Worms they placed a goose and a goat at the head of the column as emblematic of their faith and their intelligence; on the road they murdered every Jew within their reach. Many of the Jews were tortured in the most inhuman manner; thousands of men were massacred, while many others took their own lives to avoid falling into the hands of the fiendish mob.

In passing through Hungary and Bulgaria the same system of pillage and murder was adopted. These countries, having been forewarned, raised an army of 200,000 Christians with which they slaughtered over 40,000 of Walter's Crusaders, when the rest of them fled, first to the mountains, and then to Constantinople, where they were given protection by the Roman emperor. In return for this they renewed their depredations. The emperor, to get rid of them, gave them aid and quietly crossed them over to the Asiatic shore.

All Europe in Arms

All Christian Europe (for Europe was then all Christian, under the absolute will and dominion of the church) was in arms for the holy war. The motto was, the more infidels slaughtered, the more Christ would be glorified. So each of these Christian soldiers felt it a duty specially enjoined upon him to murder as many unbelievers as possible; the more the victims could be tortured, the greater the reward to the victor. Spain, Italy, and England suffered little less than France during the exit of the holy band from their territories.

When all were landed on the eastern side of the Bosporus, the lack of arms, with hunger and starvation staring them in the face, began to be realized. Much time was here spent, where thousands died from exposure and starvation; the remnant, many of them sick and emaciated, took up their march for the Holy Land.

We will not go into the details of the barbarities of this motley horde in their march through Asia Minor. Suffice it to say that, in that country, this Christian band of marauders had to contend with large numbers of Saracens, who constantly harassed the rear, and frequently gave battle to the Crusaders. In this way, and from exposure and starvation, the ranks of the Crusaders from day to day became sadly diminished; but they managed to torture and destroy thousands of the Saracens. Torture of the women and children by slow death was the delight of these pious warriors. They were driven to such straits by hunger, it is recorded, that they killed and devoured many of their own children. Quite a large body of the Crusaders finally reached the promised land, and after much delay laid siege to Jerusalem.

After long siege, and when despair reigned in their camp, a holy fraud was resorted to; they had dug up the real cross, which they reared at the head of their columns; so excited were the Christian soldiers at the sight of this emblem that a rush was made on the city.

Capture of Jerusalem

A shout was raised, and on the 15th day of July, 1099, the walls were scaled and the army entered the holy city, which contained about 100,000 people.

I will stop here for a while and let the Rev. James White finish the story. He says: 'The slaughter lasted six days, stopping only long enough to allow these pious Christians to offer up prayers. When they entered the mosque of Omar, where about one-third of the people of the city had shut themselves up for safety, the slaughter was so terrible that the horses were in blood up to their girths." We here add that these Christians also took time to sleep and eat, and that during the slaughter hundreds of babies had spears run through their bodies, which were hoisted up and carried through the streets writhing in agony. The most brutal tortures were inflicted upon women and children. A few Saracen infidels, as they were called, made their escape, all others perished. Just 433 years before this time the Saracens captured the city from the Christians; when it was surrendered to Omah, he would not even allow his army to enter the city, but offered up his prayers outside the walls, so tender was he of the feelings of the Christians.

In 1177 A.C., just sixty-eight years after the capture and slaughter by the crusading horde, the city was retaken by the Saracens under Saladin. After the surrender not a soul was injured; the Greek and Oriental Christians were allowed to remain; all others were given sixty days to prepare for departure, when they were safely escorted by the Saracen army to places of their own choice. Out of the vast hordes who enlisted in this Crusade, but a mere handful lived to get back to Europe.

Other Crusading Expeditions

There were nine or ten crusading expeditions following the first one, covering a period of over two hundred years. We will not repeat the story of the first Crusade; suffice it to say that owing to the fewer number engaged the sufferings and barbarities were not on so extensive a scale as in the first expedition. It has been estimated by historians that in all these Crusades against the infidels, more than 15,000,000 of lives were sacrificed. What for? we ask. The answer is that all this carnage and misery was to glorify Christ, and to recover his burial-place from unbelievers.

Records of the Inquisition in Evidence

We now offer in evidence the historical records of the inquisition.

Persecutions in England

In 1543, Queen Mary commenced to re-establish the old church, and in less than four years Archbishop Cranmer, Bishops Hooper and Latimer, and many other clergymen, with over three hundred of their disciples, of all ages and both sexes, were burned at the stake. During the fifteenth and sixteenth centuries large numbers were executed in England as heretics. In 1160 thirty heretics went from Germany to England to propagate their opinions; they were seized, branded on the foreheads, whipped, and thrust into the streets in the dead of winter; no one daring to relieve them, they died from cold and hunger. In 1401 a law was passed in England permitting the priests to try, condemn, and burn heretics. General slaughter by burning followed this law, says Rev. Mr. White.

At the coronation of Richard I there was a wholesale slaughter of the Jews in London by order of the Christian priests. Five hundred men, with their families, shut themselves up in a castle; the castle was besieged by a mob of Christians; the besieged killed themselves to avoid a worse death. In 1212, in England, several hundred heretics were put in prison, some of whom had their eyes put out, others had their teeth pulled out, and many of them were butchered.

The last person executed in Great Britain for heresy was Thomas Aikenhead, of Edinburgh, 1696. In 1828 an old law of England requiring the taking of the sacrament as a qualification to office was repealed.

Justin in his humanity gave all heretics three months in which to choose between exile and baptism; 70,000 pagans chose the latter and thereby became good Christians, but the Samaritans preferred the chances of war, with the result of the loss of their province, and the slaughter of 100,000 of its people.

Inquisition Established

Although the inquisition had existed in fact as far back as the eighth century, it was not established by formal decree until the meeting of the Council of Toulouse in 1229; six years before this an inquisitorial mission was created and put into the hands of the Dominicans. Pietro de Verona was the first to apply the torch. He was assassinated April 6, 1252, and afterward canonized by the church. The inquisition laws were amended or new articles added from time to time to increase the torture, and the articles went so far as to authorize the mutilation of the bodies of the dead and the punishment of the servants of the rich.

Llorente, in his "History of the Inquisition," says: 'The hand of the holy office (this is what the Christians called it) was outstretched against all; no degree in dignity in church or state, no eminence in art or science, and no purity of life could stand its madness. War was made on books of every kind;

111

700,000 volumes were burned in the temple of Serapis at Alexandria by order of the Christian Emperor Theodosius."

"In the love of Christ and his maiden mother," says Queen Isabella, "I have caused great misery, depopulated towns, districts, provinces, and kingdoms."

Llorente gives the figures 31,912 burned alive, 17,659 imprisoned and tortured, 291,450 penitents, whose torture was little better than death, a total of 341,051 during the term of his office as secretary of the inquisition. After the list of heretics had been exhausted, the Christian king and the queen of Castile turned the car of vengeance on to the Jews and Moors. For persecution of the Jews, see further on.

The age at which children could be tried, condemned, and burned was for boys ten and one-half years, and nine and one-half years for girls. None were so high in rank or power as to escape the torch; even bishops and priests suspected of leniency to heretics were subjected to the torch. It was made the duty of all to hunt up and give information; if anyone failed in this he was treated as a heretic. The suspects were, without notice, arrested and thrown into the most loathsome dungeons, where they sometimes lay for years. Occasionally they were brought out, put on the rack, and tortured for a confession or denial; if they confessed they were thrust back into the dungeon and made to do penance worse than death. All persons suspected of having any knowledge were summoned as witnesses; if they stubbornly refused to testify, or seemed to favor the accused, torture was applied to them.

A heretic could not testify in favor of a heretic, but was compelled to testify against him; the houses of all persons harboring heretics were destroyed and the inmates arrested.

Frederick Barbarossa said the sword had been given him to smite the enemies of Christ. Every official took an oath to prosecute heretics to extermination; no tie of kindred served as an excuse; the son must denounce the father, and the husband was guilty if he failed to deliver up his wife to be burned. All trials were held in secret; the accused had no opportunity of seeing his accusers; all doubts were resolved against the accused. When condemned, confiscation of property and death followed.

Heretics of both sexes and all ages were outlaws; there was no statute of limitation; the children to the second generation were disqualified from holding office; defenders of heretics were to be treated as heretics, their children disinherited and their property confiscated. Rulers and judges were required to take an oath to use their utmost endeavors to exterminate all unbelievers, under penalty of forfeiture of office; an arrest on suspicion was generally equivalent to conviction and death. Even the death of the person accused did not stop the prosecution; the trial went on against the dead heretic; his body was mutilated and his property confiscated. Even if he had died a natural death, and if at any time thereafter it was discovered that he had been a heretic, his body was taken from the grave, tried, condemned, and mutilated.

In 897 Pope Stephen VII caused the body of his predecessor (suspected of favoring a heretic), then seven months in the grave, to be dug up, dragged by the heels, and set up in the synod, where the body was tried and condemned, two fingers cut off and thrown into the Tiber, and the body reburied. In 905 this same body was again taken out of the grave by order of Sergius III, clothed in its pontifical robes, seated on the throne, tried, condemned, and beheaded, when three more fingers were cut off and thrown into the Tiber.

We cite this as a single case out of thousands who were punished after death, only to show that the doctrines of Christianity were duly promulgated and enforced.

With absolute sway over all Europe, with this machinery for conversion at its command, the church, after more than 1800 years, has succeeded in bringing into its fold as actual supporters 200,000,000, leaving 1,300,000,000 souls unconverted to Christianity.

Joseph Bonaparte, in 1808, with his army in Spain, suppressed this machinery for making Christians. Llorente, the historian, says: "After the hands of Napoleon had been taken off, the institution revived in Rome and Madrid, but its teeth were gone and it could do little but show a murderous will."

If we be told that the trial of heretics is past, that it is one of the things of the dark ages, our answer will be that heretics were burned as late as the early part of the 19th century; that the inquisition was introduced into the Spanish-American colonies, where, in Mexico, Carthagena, and Lima, it rivaled in severity that of Spain, and that within the last few years one Catholic and five Protestant clergymen have been tried in free America for heresy; but they were not burned at the stake for want of power in the church.

Persecutions in France

In 1525 the Catholics in France made general war on the Protestants and massacred great numbers of them. On the 24th of August, 1572, at the Bartholomew massacre, Scully says: "Seventy thousand French Huguenots were slaughtered, neither age nor sex was spared." In Paris alone more than 10,000 suffered death; extreme torture was the rule. This wholesale murder took place between Christians, and on the sole ground of honest difference of opinion on religious matters. In 1723, in the same country, Protestant assemblies were forbidden, churches pulled down, and death was decreed to all who should harbor heretics.

Spanish Persecutions

Rev. James White, in his "Eighteen Centuries," says: "In the thirteenth century came the order in Spain for the first crusade against heretics in the province of Languedoc, instigated by Dominic Guzman, and under the command of Simon de Montfort. To his standard flocked the devout from all parts of Europe. The pious Guzman gave orders, saying: 'Ravish every field, slay every human being, and the blessing will be with you.' Soon word was sent that the crusaders could not distinguish orthodox from heretics; the answer came back: 'Slaughter all; God will take care of his own.'" St. Dominic, at the commencement of the carnage, wrote the pope regretting that he had so far been unable to destroy more than 20,000 heretics. Mr. White further says: "Over a quarter of a million victims was the result of the slaughter for heresy in one province."

Persecution of the Jews

When the supply of heretics and infidels gave out, the persecution of the Jews commenced at wholesale.

It will be remembered that Christ was a Jew, that he followed in the wake of his early teachers, preaching the doctrines of Judaism, and finally, in common with several others, claimed to be the long-looked-for Jewish Messiah. His followers were for the first century looked upon by the Romans as a sect of the Jews, while by the Hebrews they were characterized as Nazarenes; nor was it until the beginning of the second century that they threw ofif the old coat of Judaism and took on that of Christians. Now, as children of Israel, having in number outgrown the parent stock, and having learned to despise their ancestors, let us look at the action of the child toward its parent.

The persecution of the despised race, as the Christians called the Jews, began at an early date. Finding the Jews too stubborn, the followers of the meek and lowly turned their attention to the world of pagans. As it is not the purpose of this work to go into details, we will pass over the first nine centuries of Christian sway, with the statement that during that early time Christian doctrines had not fully ripened, the true Christian spirit had not fully developed, nor were the nations of Europe so far sunk in barbarism as to tolerate the enforcement of true Christianity by fire and sword. That time was reached about the close of the tenth century, when the Christian church held all Europe in its grasp; kings and emperors trembled at the edicts and bulls of the vicegerent of Christ. As the octopus holds its victim in his death struggle, so the priest held the lives and liberty of the people and their property in his clerical fangs. When the mythological ruler belched forth his decrees and hurled his anathemas, all was as silent as the grave; science had been nipped in the bud, no writings in conflict or antagonism to the church were allowed; all books, before publication, had to undergo inspection by the church, and if found obnoxious in the slightest degree, were destroyed. All attempts by the people to acquire general knowledge were stamped upon, unless conducted under the supervision of the church. It was under this state of things that the humane and benevolent spirit of Christianity dawned upon the followers of Abraham and Moses, by burning, roasting, torturing, maiming, and finally putting to death more than one-half of the Hebrew race.

We forbear going into the refined Christian devices of torture, except to a limited extent, lest we shock the holy church and its mythologians, and thereby create a tendency to lessen their power, diminish their private incomes and luxurious benefices and maintenance.

It is well-established history that in France alone, thousands of Jews were burned at the stake. On one occasion one hundred and sixty men, women, and children were bound hand and foot and thrown into a ditch, wood was piled on them, and the torch applied, while numbers of priests stood by with uplifted hands calling on their Savior to witness the suffering of the unbelieving Jews; whole families were burned in this funeral pyre for the reason that the pious Christians could not see them separated.

Only few and far between, says one historian, were the Christian monarchs who rose above the barbarities of the church.

From the eleventh to the fourteenth centuries, says another historian, the history of the Jews is a succession of massacres. Philip Augustus confiscated their property and banished them from France.

Louis IX, a very pious prince, says an historian, confiscated a third of the property of the Jews for the benefit of his own soul, and at the same time issued an edict for the destruction of their sacred books by fire; in this fire four cartloads of the Talmud were consumed.

A large share of this confiscated property was given over to the priests, to intercede with Christ for the salvation of the monarch's soul.

In the reign of Philip the Fair, 1306 A.C., the Jews (having returned to France) were again expelled from the country with the usual accompaniment of cruelty, says another author. The financial condition of the country became embarrassed, and the Jews were permitted to return.

In 1321, a religious epidemic having seized the faithful, an uprising took place, when the poor, unfortunate Jews were, without regard to age or sex, indiscriminately slaughtered. In their flight and frenzy the Jews at Verdan threw their children into the streets to appease the infuriated Christian mob. In the following year in whole provinces every Jew was burned. Finally, in 1395, they were indiscriminately banished from middle France.

In the time of the first crusading spirit, in the cities of Treves, Metz, Mainz, Worms, Spires, Strasburg, and other smaller places, the streets were deluged with the blood of the Jews and other unbelievers, at the hands of these pious warriors.

The Jews were expelled from Vienna in 1196; from Mecklenburg in 1225; from Breslau in 1226; from Brandenburg in 1243; from Frankfort in 1241; from Munich in 1285; from Nuremburg in 1380; from Prague in 1391, and from Ratisbon in 1476.

From 1346 to 1350 the Jews were murdered by thousands, until the race in Germany became nearly extinct.

In Switzerland the Christians commenced to persecute the Jews about the middle of the 14th century, and in the 15th they were expelled from the principal cities in that country.

In Spain, during the sixth and seventh centuries, the Jews were persecuted without mercy. When the Moors invaded Spain, the Jews lent a helping hand, so glad were they to escape Christian tortures; they were made equals wherever the Moors held sway, while in the Christian provinces the persecutions were carried on in that refined manner known only to the followers of the cross.

In 1391-92, in five provinces, held by the followers of Christ, untold numbers of Jews were murdered and their property was confiscated to the church. Escape, says one historian, was possible only through flight to Africa or by accepting baptism at the point of the sword. The number of converts so made at that time has been estimated at 200,000.

Such a vast number of stubborn Jews, so quickly converted and thereby brought under the mild influence of Christianity, must have been as gratifying to the followers of Christ as assuring to the adherents of Moses.

To say the least of it, this process is much more expeditious, if not more soothing and lasting, than the tedious mode of reasoning; besides, it is in strict accordance with the teachings and rules of the mythologian.

In speaking of this affair, one writer says: 'The fate of the Jews in Spain during the fifteenth century beggars description." He further says: "Persecutions, violent conversions, massacre, the torture of the inquisition, we read of nothing else! At length the hour of final horror came, when in 1492 an edict was issued from those pious rulers, Ferdinand and Isabella, by which the Jews were given four months within which to leave the country empty-handed, to accept baptism, or to suffer death."

It being claimed by the priests that the teachings of Christ forbade the spilling of human blood, to avoid the breach of their master's precepts, these pious men ordered their victims to be burned to death. This the Jews well knew to be the fate of those who failed to leave their homes and country or become Christians. The numbers who are said to have chosen to abandon the country in which they and their ancestors had resided for seven centuries have been variously estimated at from three to eight hundred thousand. Every person in Spain was forbidden to shelter or feed them in their transit, and almost every Christian country shut its doors against them.

As they were forbidden to take away with them gold or silver, their condition was heart-rending in the extreme. All except the devout Christians, and, it is said, even some of these, shed tears over the departure of these wretched beings; but from that divine order of priesthood not a tear dropped, nor was a moan heard to disturb the peace and tranquility of their Christian souls. Some of the fugitives ventured into Italy and France, but by far the greater number turned their faces toward Morocco.

Of all the vast hordes who left Spain, more than one-half died from exposure and hunger before reaching their destination. Some 80,000 bought of the Christian sovereign of Portugal a stop-over privilege until they could earn money enough to go on.

After the lapse of the time for their exit, many lingered, being unable to get away. King Emanuel, in the tenderness of his Christian heart, sold into slavery many of the more common Jews, and by an edict he ordered all the children under fourteen years of age, of the better class, to be taken from their parents and turned over to the Christian brothers to be brought up in the true faith.

This piece of refined cruelty drove many of the mothers to destroy their offspring rather than let them fall into the hands of their persecutors. Those who accepted forced baptism, but who for the most part secretly adhered to their old faith, were constantly on the rack of torture.

The Reformation — Luther and Calvin

It will not do to say that these persecutions were all by the Catholics. During most of the time they were in progress, there was no other Christian church, but even after the Protestants gained the ascendency, there was no abatement of these cruelties. Luther and Calvin, while claiming the utmost liberty of conscience for themselves, denied it to all others. Luther denounced Copernicus, the astronomer, and, says his biographer, he looked with a favorable eye on the adoption of violent measures for the conversion of the Jews and others.

He was extremely vile in the epithets which he applied to men of learning, calling them such names as locusts, caterpillars, frogs, lice, etc. To Aristotle he applied the epithets of devil, prince of darkness, beast, impostor, liar, etc.

No one can mistake the character of the man from the use of such language.

As for Calvin, after he had fled from place to place to escape arrest and punishment for his opinions, he finally settled in Geneva, where he gained such influence and control as to establish ecclesiastical over civil law, thereby giving him power over that city. In 1555 he banished the officials for attempting to maintain civil institutions; to do this was, to Calvin, heresy.

A controversy having arisen between Calvin and Servetus on the dogma of the trinity, and the latter having fled to escape the wrath of the former, Calvin sent his emissaries to Vienna, where, in conjunction with the Catholics, he had Servetus arrested, brought to Geneva, tried for heresy, condemned, taken out on a hill near the city, tied to a stake, green wood piled around him and a fire applied, where Servetus was slowly roasted to death on Oct. 26, 1553. Shortly after this, Jerome Bolses raised a point as to Calvin's doctrine of predestination. To this Calvin told Bolses that no dissenting opinions would be tolerated; Bolses, not recanting, was banished from the city.

An author, in speaking of the hardships of the Jews, says: "That the Reformation gave no aid to the Jews is only too plain, from the fact that in many parts of Protestant Germany their lot became harder than before."

The Jews were driven out of Protestant Bavaria in 1553; out of Brandenburg in 1573. In the Protestant city of Hamburg, in 1730, they were persecuted in the most inhuman manner; and during the whole of the seventeenth and a part of the eighteenth centuries Protestant Germany increased its persecutions. This author concludes by saying: "What really caused the change in their favor was the great uprising of human reason that marked the middle of the eighteenth century."

Notwithstanding that Luther was petulant, dogmatical, and intolerant, he had some good qualities; but as to Calvin, his biography stands in the way of saying anything good of him; among his crimes that of the murder of Servetus can never be excused.

At the present time the Jews have had their property confiscated and are being driven out of Russia by the Christian emperor of that country, on the ground that they cannot and do not believe in the dogmas of Christianity. All who will accept baptism and become Christians are exempt from this cruel edict.

The Puritans fled from Europe to America to avoid persecution for religious opinions, but no sooner had they set foot on the soil of New England than they enacted the most cruel penal laws and enforced them on all dissenters.

Prof. Huxley says: "If we could only see in one view the torrents of hypocrisy and cruelty, the lies, the slaughter, the violation of every obligation of honesty which have flowed from this source along the course of the history of Christian nations, our imagination of hell would pale beside the vision." He further says: "And the wolf would play the same havoc now if it could only get its bloodstained jaws free from the muzzle imposed by the secular arm." Yes, the clerical wolf lets go only when he is forced to do so, and then only drops one bone at a time.

Under the enlightened influence of reason, science, and growing humanity, fiery Hades has fallen into disrepute, and the more enlightened of the clergy have adopted courses of lectures instead of sermons wherein the torments of hell used to be portrayed from the pulpits in all their hideousness.

Dark Ages

We now offer in evidence the shadow of the dark ages, covering a period of a thousand years, from the fifth to the fifteenth century, when the church held absolute dominion and sway over every government and people of Europe. Under its exercise of power, religion took the place of learning; monasteries and cloisters took the place of colleges; monks, bishops, and priests took the place of statesmen; ecclesiastical dogmas the place of civil law; the thumbscrew, sharpened spikes, and other devices such only as devout Christians could invent, took the place of free thought; prayers and images took the place of science and art, libraries were burned, and all reading was forbidden.

The first society for the promotion of physical science, founded at Naples by Baptista Porta, and the Accademia del Ciemento, established at Florence, 1657, were suppressed by the ecclesiastical authorities.

Galileo, for having committed the crime of discovering that the earth revolved on its axis, Copernicus for having discovered that the planets revolved around the sun, and Bruno for having announced the plurality of worlds, were each told by the church that such things were against the Bible, and could not be promulgated under pain of death. Bruno was burned at the stake for refusing to recant. Vanini, one of Italy's brightest scholars, for the offense of being the author of some philosophical works, was arrested at Taurisona, tried, and convicted of heresy, tied to a stake, told to put out his tongue, and on refusal, it was drawn out with irons and cut off; a fire was kindled around him, when his sufferings were relieved by death, July 9, 1619.

Hypatia, one of the most refined ladies of Alexandria, a teacher of mathematics and philosophy to the most learned men of the Roman Empire, was, by order of Bishop Cyril, stripped naked by a gang of monks, who dragged her from the academy through the streets, took her into a church, where they murdered her, after which they scraped the flesh off the bones with shells and burned it. This piece of Christian refinement took place in the year 414 A.C., and was, as Cyril said, done as a warning to others not to teach doctrines antagonistic to the church.

Following this act, and in obedience to the church. Justinian, the devout emperor, closed all of the philosophical schools of Athens. We here offer these humane acts in evidence in support of the almost daily assertions of the pope and his satellites that their church has always been the friend and supporter of liberty of speech, freedom of action, and human progress.

Crime and religion are fellow-companions; science, progress, and humanity were dead; the church was happy, while monks, priests, bishops, and clergymen shouted psalms, hymns, prayers, and doxologies over the grave.

Witch-burning by the Church

'Thou shalt not suffer a witch to live." — Exodus xxii, 18.

"A man, also a woman, that hath a familiar spirit, or that is a wizard, shall surely be put to death." — Leviticus xx, 27.

"And Saul had put away those that had familiar spirits and the wizards out of the land." — I Samuel xxviii, 3.

Let the following records tell how well the church obeyed these commands and precepts of the holy Bible.

In spite of Christianity the world having outgrown the inquisition, it was left for the church to hunt up another class of victims, and this it was not slow to do.

It now turns its shafts of vengeance and pours its vials of pious wrath on another innocent class, denominated witches; a class supposed to be in league with the devil against the church and all good Christians.

The following comprises a few of the first pages of this record:

In 1484 Pope Innocent issued a bull to punish witches; under this decree tens of thousands were burned alive, says Bishop Hutchinson. On May 30, 143 1, Joan of Arc was burned at the stake. In three months of the year 1524 five hundred were burned in Germany. The total number burned in Germany alone, says Mr. Hutchinson, reached the incredible number of 100,000. In 1520 an incredible number were burned in France, the figures not given. Nine hundred were burned between 1580 and 1595 at Wurzburg. At Leinheim thirty were burned in four years, out of a population of six hundred. In 1634 the parish priest of London was burned on a charge of bewitching a whole convent. In 1654 twenty women were burned at Beslague. In 1749 Renata was burned at Wurtenburg. On Jan. 17, 1775, at Kalis, Poland, nine women were burned on a charge of bewitching, and thereby rendering land unproductive. In 1664 Sir Matthew Hale burned two. In 1670 eighteen were burned in Essex, England. From 1775 to 1777 nine were burned in Northampton, England. In 1716 Mrs. Hix and her daughter, aged nine years, were hung as witches at Huntingdon.

The historian Harrington estimates the total number of witches burned in England at 30,000.

Mr. Henry Charles Lee, in his "History of the Inquisition," says that Protestants and Catholics rivaled each other in the madness of the hour; witches were no longer burned in ones and twos, but in scores and hundreds. He further says that the Bishop of Geneva burned five hundred in three months; that a Bishop of Ramburg burned six hundred; a Bishop of Wurzburg burned nine hundred; that eight hundred were condemned in a body at Savoy; that in the spring of 1556 the Archbishop of Treves burned one hundred and eighteen women, and that Bishop Paramo boasted that in a century and a half the holy office had burned at least 50,000.

Estimates of the total number of witches put to death by the church run from seven and a half to fourteen millions; nine millions, says one author, would be a conservative statement.

In Salem, Mass., nineteen were hanged, eight others were condemned, fifty confessed and were pardoned.

Will some kind teacher of divinity advise us to whom credit is due for the destruction of so many cruel witches? Shall it be given to Jehovah, to the Bible, to the mythologian, or to the general humane spirit of the Christian system — a system resting on its code, the Bible, a book made up largely of a heterogeneous mass of absurdities, contradictions, childish jargon, myths, legends, and supreme nonsense; a sublime production, well worthy the genius and combined wisdom of popes, priests, bishops, and ecumenical councils; a book extremely edifying and instructive to the devout because of its incomprehensible vagaries, giving scope to a vast number of speculations and theories, ending in guesses, disagreements, interminable disputes and quarrels, and the slaughter of millions of innocent men, women, and children.

The Pope and the Priesthood

The bull of Hildebrand, Pope Gregory VII, promulgated 1075, specially directed against Henry IV of Germany, among other matters, contains the following provisions: The Roman church was founded by God. The Roman pontiff is universal. The pope may use the insignia of empire. He is the only person whose feet are kissed by all princes; he may depose emperors. No scriptures or books are canonical without his authority. His decrees can be annulled by no one. He may be judged by no one. No one may dare to condemn a person who appeals to the pope. The Roman church has never erred, nor ever, by the witness of scripture, shall err, to all eternity. The pope may absolve subjects from their allegiance. Let it not be forgotten that the church never changes; its decrees and bulls once promulgated are always in force, and apply equally to all Christians, Protestants as well as Catholics, and we must remember that the Roman hierarchy has never faltered in the use of its powers to enforce its will. Its sole object is dominion. When it deems it expedient it suspends its decrees. Whenever it has had the power, it has used it to depose and excommunicate emperors and kings and drive their people into rebellion against the civil authorities. Pope Gregory VII spent his official life in attempting to overthrow the civil governments of Europe. He succeeded in driving the people of Germany into rebellion against Henry IV, and he died in exile fighting civil society. We must remember that the Jesuitical Society is the arm of the papacy; that it possesses great learning, policy, and address, and is full of craft and deceit; that in countries where it has been established, it has secured, by art and diplomacy, vast tracts of land which it has used to foster and fortify its position. Mexico, the Central and South American states, and most of the states of Europe, for self-protection, found it necessary to banish this people from their countries and confiscate their property. After being driven from other lands, the Society of Jesus planted itself in the United States, where in conjunction with the Roman priesthood, it is scheming to establish Romanism on the ruins of American civil institutions. While this is going on under orders from the banks of the Tiber, the great body of American Protestant clergymen are demanding that their God be put into the Federal Constitution. Not content with this, they are making the air resound with their babbling clamors that their nefarious Sunday blue laws be adopted by the State and Federal governments, and thereby deprive the people, for at least one day of the week, of their natural rights. This same doleful howl is also going up from the pulpits of England. We ask, in all seriousness, if the time has not come for free action, as well as free thought, if the American people are to retain the liberties vouchsafed to them by the sword of Washington and the pen of Jefferson.

And here the question comes back once more, this time from, the graves of over 30,000,000 of innocent men, women, and children, surrounded by burning fagots or tortured with every instrument that Christian ingenuity and zeal could devise, whether the world would not have been better off if the church had never existed.

Having disposed of this humane branch of the case, and while waiting the verdict of the country, let us look into some of the wise acts of the church and its priests.

Trial and Punishment of Quadrupeds and Insects by the Church

The mythologian, having exhausted his powers in the punishment of mankind, turns with delight to a new field of action, where without let or hindrance he can hurl his ecclesiastical shafts at the lower order of the animal world. Unlike the humanity of the poor Hindu, who is taught by his religion to extend kindness to the beast, the reptile, and even the insect, the teacher of Christianity can see no reason why, if man is punished, the quadruped and insect should not be.

As this new field opened a wide range for the display of the intellectual powers of the priest, he established his ecclesiastical court for the trial, condemnation, and punishment of bulls, pigs, reptiles, and insects.

Incredible as it may appear to the people in this enlightened age, it is nevertheless historically true, that from the 12th to the 16th century, the lower animals and even insects were tried by the ecclesiastical tribunals; some were condemned and executed, while others were excommunicated.

In 1410 the Bishop of Laon (France), after a regular trial, pronounced an injunction against caterpillars and field mice. Full details exist of the trial of a hog in 1494, wherein it is set forth that the hog was duly sentenced, and strangled on a gibbet. In 1497 a sow was tried, condemned, and beaten to death for having eaten off a child's chin in the village of Chroroune; in 1386 Bishop Folais condemned a sow to be mutilated and thereafter hung. Numerous cases of the trial of bulls are reported.

In 1587 proceedings were instituted against beetles for ravages in the vineyards of St. Julian; the beetles having disappeared, the proceedings were dismissed; having reappeared forty years thereafter, proceedings were revived.

In the "History of the Swiss Reformation," by De Ruchat, many such trials appear, wherein full details of the proceedings are given, too silly and ridiculous to merit contempt. In one case the trial was of cockroaches at Lansome;

after trial the insects were condemned in the name of the holy trinity and the blessed Virgin.

The same author narrates a case wherein a miraculous image was a witness against a pig.

It will be remembered that a few years ago the great state of Minnesota was overrun with grasshoppers; they seemed to come up out of the very bowels of the earth, and were so numerous as to threaten the destruction of every green thing in the land. The people sought every means to get rid of them, to no avail. The opportune moment had arrived when the specially ordained agents of Jehovah were to take a hand in the fray; notices were sent to the clergymen everywhere, a day was fixed for the general onslaught, by prayers and anathemas; the day dawned, the trial commenced, when over two thousand mythologians hurled from their rostrums the sacred javelin until, as we may imagine, not a hopper was left to tell the tale of that direful conflict. Whether the sun stood still to allow these Joshuas to finish their work, we are not advised, but we may imagine that the sun went down on a scene of desolation.

After such evidence, who will doubt the potency of prayer in the extermination of pestilential hoppers, licentious bugs and unbelievers?

Whatever may be said as to the fact that these hoppers did not have their day in court, that they were not assigned counsel by this clerical tribunal, that they did not have an opportunity to face their accusers or to cross-examine witnesses, it will not be denied that these hoppers were tried by their peers.

Since writing the foregoing, we are advised by telegraph that the devout believers at the foot of Mount Etna are praying to stop the flow of lava, which in obedience to the law of gravitation is running down the mountain.

In closing this branch of the subject it may truthfully be said that for what liberty we now possess, we are largely indebted to the divisions and dissensions in the church, and the indifference manifested by so many of its lay members, who give no thought, heed, or concern to the making of proselytes. They have nothing to gain, hence their indifference. Not so with the priest or mythologian, whose influence, authority, power, and salary depend on the number of votaries he can draw into his web. It is he who, from the dawn of the persecutions to the present time, directed and carried on all the inhuman and barbarous persecutions that have so signally marked the progress of the church and the spirit of Christianity, at the expense of liberty, knowledge, and humanity.

The ordinary mythologian lives to-day in the bygone ages; progress with him is an impossibility; his world of thought is confined to his Bible and its teachings. Standing on this vast pedestal of clerical arrogance, he unfolds his hymn-book and sings psalms to the credulous multitude. With his prayers he can change the laws of the universe, bring down the wrath of heaven, destroy grasshoppers and other pestilential insects, and cause copious showers to

123

descend on the parched-up earth. He listens to the talk between Eve and the serpent as to the propriety of eating an apple. He sees the Almighty walking in the shade, and hears him call to Adam. He is present at the building of the ark. After the storm has subsided, he helps Noah out of the ship, builds the sacrificial fire,, and smells a sweet savor. He knows that as the child bloweth his soap bubble to float on the soft air, so the great "I am," by a single breath, brought forth from the fathomless realms of nothingness our earth, with its attendant satellites, the sun to give light to man by day, and the moon and stars to illuminate his course by night. He knows that all these things were created in a single day He remembers the fall of Adam, and knows that Moses wrote the Pentateuch, and that it was written by the command of the Almighty on Mount Sinai. He was present when the children of Israel came out of Egypt, and knows that Pharaoh and his army were lost in the Red Sea.

All of these things, and several others, this primate knows, because his Bible tells him so, and this book, being the work of inspiration, is necessarily true, and all science in conflict with its teachings is to him false.

There is another class, the explanatory homo, who, in attempting to retain his power and influence over the multitude, is trying to explain away and adjust the conflicts between his Bible and science. Poor fellow, he deserves our sympathy, for his task is a hard one.

Lastly, there is a third class, which seeing no escape from the deadly conflict between science and religion, is throwing off its clerical robes, and its members one by one are taking their places in the field of science. Thus it will be seen that even the mythologian has not escaped the laws of nature. He first made his appearance in the post-tertiary period as a simple protoplastic Pator, from which evolved the conjuror, the soothsayer, the diviner, the prophet, the rabbi, the priest, and the theologian; at all times, and in each stage, a mediator between Gods and men. Having thus fulfilled the laws of evolution, and reached an age of science in which no oracle can live, he is ready to deposit his bones with those of other extinct mammals.

In his "Service of Man," J. C. Morison, speaking from an English standpoint, very properly says: "The general tendency of opinion shows that in the near future Christianity must disappear from among the more advanced populations of the globe, for it is no longer tenable by educated people."

Mythology or Hindustan

Brahma, whose name is used in the masculine, feminine, and neuter, stands at the head of the Gods of the Hindu pantheon — the soul of the universe. He is called in Sanscrit. Trimurti, and in his three genders, or phases, he is Brahma, Vishnu, and Siva. Resolved back into a unit, like the Christian trinity, the three become one, and that one is Brahma or Trimurti.

Brahma represents the principles of creation, preservation, and destruction.

Vishnu is sometimes called the creator, and as such is represented by the sun in its onward course through the heavens, when he takes on the character of the Egyptian trinity at dawn, meridian, and setting. Vishnu, like Jehovah, is described as allowing a portion of himself, in the form of a man, begotten by Brahma and incarnate, to descend to earth for the salvation of mankind.

The Hindu code of morals, or religious teaching, closely resembles the teachings of Buddha and Confucius.

The Hindus have a legend that, Vishnu having fallen asleep, the demon Hayagaiva stole the Vedas; Vishnu assumes the form of a fish, reveals to Menu a coming flood to destroy the world, tells Menu that there will be sent to him a ship, and orders that he take animals and seeds into the ship. The deluge came as foretold and destroyed all life on the earth, and when the flood subsided, Vishnu taught Menu all that was pure and good.

Mythology of Ancient Persia

Zoroaster, or Zarathustra, the founder or reformer of Persian mythology, is supposed to have been an Iranian, born in Bactria. Like Christ and Mohammed, he left no writings; his teachings were reduced to writing some time after his death, by his disciples at different times; amended and modified at a much later date. The date of his birth is unknown; there is a wide divergence of opinion on this point, but from the best authority we have, the time of his birth was not later than 1800 B. C. His teachings, or supposed teachings, are contained in the Zend-Avesta, or Avesta.

Zoroaster claimed, or it is claimed for him, as for all other founders of religions, that these sacred writings came directly from the lips of Ahura Mazda (Ormuzd). This divinity told Zoroaster that he once conferred all power on Yima, who ruled the earth for a thousand years, during which time there was no death, all was perfect happiness; that Yima then sinned, fell from grace, and was cast out into the world of darkness, where he, in the form of a serpent, wandered over the earth, enticing men away from Ahura Mazda.

Zoroaster, like Christ, was taken up into a mountain by Yima, the evil one, and offered the whole earth if he would turn from his religion.

Dr. Haug, Windischmann, Spiegel, et al, say that the belief in immortality was one of the principal dogmas of Zoroaster, believed by many to have been borrowed from Persia by the Christians. These authors further say that the Jewish and Christian notions of a Messiah were borrowed from Mosiosh, who occupied a similar position in the mythology of Zoroaster. He, like Christ, was begotten by a God, and his last office was to awake the dead and bring them to judgment.

Chinese Philosophy and Transmigration

Buddha, the Chinese philosopher, was born in Hindustan; the time of his birth is unknown. Writers have speculated on the time, varying from 600 to 2000 years B. C. When we know that his teachings had attained a foothold in India and China as early as 550 B. C, the time of his birth could not have been later than about 1000 B.C.

In thus giving 1000 years B. C. as the date of the birth of Buddha, I am not unmindful of the fact that probably a majority of modern writers fix that event at from five to six hundred years B. C, but they give no satisfactory reasons therefor, while Penny, in his encyclopaedia, fixes a thousand years, and says that numerous recent Chinese and Japanese writers concur on from twelve to ten hundred years, and that the writers who give earlier dates confound some one of the early sages with Buddha, and that those who give the latest dates confound some one of the later Buddhas with the founder of the sect.

It is said that he (Buddha) was a prince by the name of Siddhartha; his mother died in his infancy; he was reared by his aunt, Gautama, hence he is sometimes called Gautama, and at others Buddha, signifying wisdom and goodness.

Chinese tradition says he was born of a virgin named Maya, amid great miracles; was in later life tempted by an evil spirit, called Mara, which he defied. He commenced his teachings in his native country, where he encountered the enmity of the Brahmans, in consequence of which he fled into northwestern India, where he successfully propagated his philosophy for about forty years, when he died. He left no writings.

After his death his principal followers met in council, and proceeded to reduce his teachings to waiting.

Buddhism rests on human existence, and the philosophy which prevailed among the Brahmans.

The doctrine of transmigration, in all its essential features similar to that which prevailed in Egypt and India, was in all probability borrowed some time after the death of Buddha, since which time the Chinaman has been taught that after death he is to pass through some or all of the lower animals, according to his fitness; when he is to become a perfect being.

Buddha claimed, or his followers claimed for him, that he had passed through all these stages of existence, and finally attained a state of perfection.

The Chinaman is now taught that this state of things is brought about by, and is the result of, the inherent force of matter under general laws.

Contrary to general belief, Buddhism recognizes no supreme being; hence all Buddhist nations and peoples, says an eminent writer, are essentially atheists. In this respect Buddhism differs from Brahmanism, which asserts an universal spirit in nature.

The Buddhist philosophy teaches and enjoins general love of all mankind and even the lower order of animals; to love our enemies, to abstain from even defensive warfare; avoid all vice, inculcate virtue; be obedient to parents, provide food, shelter, and comfort for man and animals, respect all religions, and persecute no dissenters. Honor your own faith, and do not slander that of others, is a Buddhist maxim.

Universal charity and toleration of all other beliefs, says an historian, is one of the Buddhist cardinal virtues, and he says the persecution of Christians in China does not grow out of religion, but is the result of the meddlesome character of the missionaries.

However much the Christians took from the pagan nations, it is quite certain that they did not borrow from the Chinese, or others, either charity or toleration.

Asoka, king of Magadha, for a time persecuted the followers of Buddha, but thereafter, like Paul, he by a miracle became converted, and like Constantine, made the new teachings national.

Buddhism is taught in China, Japan, Ceylon, Siam, Burmah, Nepal, and Tibet, to 450,000,000 of people.

After the death of Gautama Buddha, his disciples, about 250 B.C., reduced to writing the teachings of their master, thereby forming a canon of sacred writings.

Some time after this, tradition, contrary to the belief and teachings of Buddha, assigned him a place at the head of immortal spirits, and threw around his birth and life a network of legends, wherein it is said that he was conceived of a virgin by the soul of the universe; that while the virgin was on her way to visit some friends, she gave birth to Buddha beneath the shade of a Bo-tree (holy tree), over which spirits hovered to protect him; that sages from afar off came and worshiped him; and that when a small boy he surpassed his teachers in knowledge. From the age of nineteen until twenty-nine tradition loses sight of him.

At the age of twenty-nine Buddha goes into the wilderness for study and meditation, where he is tempted by an evil spirit called Mara, who offers him the kingdoms of the four quarters of the earth to forego his philosophical teachings; he spurns the offer, and seeks his disciples in the mountains, where they renew their devotion to their old teacher. He instructs them to separate, go to the four quarters of the earth and preach his gospel of truth, virtue, and purity, until all ends in Nirvana (eternal death), the home of peace beyond the ocean of existence, to the shore of salvation, where death ends all suffering and all existence.

Buddha goes to Sena, in the desert, to commune with the hermit philosophers, who warn him of approaching enemies.

In answer to questions of these hermits, Buddha says: "If they revile me, I will make no reply; if they strike me, I will not resent the injury; and if they kill me, death is no evil, but eternal rest."

127

His disciples, about 250 B.C., reduced to writing his sayings, among which was: "When I have passed away, do not think that Buddha has left you, for he is still in your midst; revere my memory, love one another, remember that which causes life causes death and decay, let your minds be filled with truth, and do good to all mankind."

The story put into the mouth of Christ by the authors of the gospels is quite a good copy of the teachings of Buddha, except that Buddha recognized no God or future existence.

Buddha possessed all the learning of his day, and his followers were of the highest order of intelligence.

Gautama Buddha taught the plurality of worlds, that nothing is eternal, that one life passes and another takes its place, that the higher forms evolve from the lower, and that all things are the result of natural law.

One of this great philosopher's cardinal doctrines was to be kind and tender, not only to all mankind, but to beasts and even insects, to injure no living thing, and revile no religious teachings.

While the atheists of China were following the teachings of this great humanitarian, extending the utmost toleration to all counter-opinions, nursing and feeding sick animals, going out of their way to avoid treading on insects, and even filtering the water they drank, lest they should swallow and thereby destroy the lives of animalcules, the Christian priests were torturing and murdering millions of innocent men, women, and children.

The priests of Rome were too busy in forging the biography of their mythical Christ, and copying therein the legends concerning Buddha, to even think of observing any of his humanitarian teachings.

Kong-fu-tse, or Confucius, the Chinese sage, was born June 19, 551 B.C. at Shang Ping, in the little kingdom of Loo. His real name was Kong, but his disciples added fu-tse, signifying teacher. He taught pure philosophy, morals, rhetoric, and politics, rejecting all supernatural things and religions as unworthy of consideration. Having been asked whether any one sentence could express the conduct most fitting for one's whole life, he replied: "Do not unto others what you would not have them do to you." After traveling over a large part of the empire teaching his philosophy, he died at seventy years of age.

After his death temples were erected to his memory in nearly all of the cities. He recognized no supreme power outside of nature and nature's laws in the universe; doubted the existence of mind in matter; looked on the universe as existing from eternity, and self-sustaining.

His five cardinal virtues were universal charity, impartial justice, conformity to established rules, rectitude in heart and mind, and pure sincerity. He, as a materialist, appealed to practical men, and claimed no knowledge as to future existence. His disciples, unlike those of founders of religions, were of the highest and most intellectual order; in fact, says a biographer, the entire literary class were his followers.

Notwithstanding the non-recognition of a supreme intelligence, the populace in China, as elsewhere, must have something to venerate, and so there grew up in later years a system of worship of heroes and demigods, and along with this system, naturally grew up a priesthood, which, like that class everywhere, claimed to be able to commune with the spirits of departed heroes and friends. Disagreements and dissensions having sprung up, the fabric broke up into three parts, the Buddhists, Confucians, and Taoists, all of whom sacrificed to the sun, moon, mountains, and rivers, and offered up prayers to the departed souls of great men, Joss being worshiped as a great general. Their prayers, like those of some Christian sects, have been reduced to fixed forms, consisting of such phrases as "I take refuge with Buddha"; "I take refuge with Confucius."

In the course of time a device, or machine, was invented in the form of a hollow cylinder, on different parts of which the prayer was written; the cylinder was turned by a crank bringing to view the prayer. Some of these machines were ponderous, and were set in the roadway for passers-by, who by a kick of the foot turned up the prayer. Others were small, and were carried around by the devotee.

Whatever may be thought of this device, it is certainly just as potent and effectual as, and much more convenient than, the Christian system.

Buddhism was introduced into Japan 552 A. C, where it underwent some modification by a mixture with the worship of the great sun Goddess.

There, as in China, the intelligent class are atheists, following Buddha and Confucius.

Mythology of Egypt

Having heretofore considered the Gods of Egypt, we will here speak only of its system of morals and religion. An Egyptologist has said that this people attained an extraordinary degree of perfection. They believed in a future existence; that at death the good and bad deeds were weighed in scales; Toth stood by to keep the account. If the good deeds preponderated, the soul entered at once the boat of the sun; otherwise the unhappy being began a round of transmigrations through the bodies of animals. The length of time in the transit, and the number and kind of animals in which the spirit lived, depended on its depravity at death. If after a long sojourn there were found incurable souls, complete annihilation took place. The Egyptian code, like that of India, Persia, and China, but unlike that of the Christians, required good works, instead of mere faith and belief. Egyptian religion required all to be industrious, to feed the hungry, relieve the oppressed, do no violence, hold no malice, be just and true, offer no offense, oppress no widow, imprison no one, allow no one to go hungry, and grant no favors to the rich over the poor.

Mythology of Greece

The fundamental ideas of the religion of Greece were brought from the northwest of India, which is believed to have been the cradle of the Hellenic stock. In later years Egypt and Phoenicia brought in their Gods, and to some extent modified the religion. The adding of new divinities created no conflict; all were blended into one harmonious system. Justice toward all men lay at the foundation of their religion. They entertained a vague idea of a future existence, which was more strongly marked when applied to great men and heroes. Extraordinary crimes were punished in Hades, or the more terrible Tartarus. They had a council of twelve divinities, at the head of which stood Zeus, Poseidon, and Apollo. Numerous other and lesser Gods filled up the Pantheon, many of whom were mortal heroes, sprung from the embrace of Gods and the beautiful daughters of men. The religion on the whole was bright and joyous, and among the mildest and most tolerant of the ancient creeds. The office of the priest was limited to the care of the temples and sacred property, the recitation of formulas, and the expounding of the divine will, expressed in oracles.

They had a trinity, says Sir Gardner Wilkinson, consisting of Osiris, the masculine principle, Isis, the feminine, and Orus, the offspring.

Comparison of the Different Religions

There is a close resemblance in all the systems, showing a continuous unbroken line of descent from the earliest to the latest.

In all except Judaism there are numerous divinities, the Christians having the least number; in all there is a clearly defined head, or supreme ruler, who not only rules over men, but over all lesser Gods. They all have a dual principle, good and evil; the good is controlled by celestial beings, and the evil is with them all represented by a serpent. The strangest part of it is, that they all have a trinity; and that trinity, with all of them, is capable of uniting itself into one and dissolving itself back into three beings at will; and in most of them one of the personages of the triad has been begotten of a beautiful woman by one of the Gods.

In this mythological category we have not included the Chinese, for, strictly speaking, theirs is not a religion, unless we can call the worship of departed ancestors by the more ignorant, a religion.

The systems taught by Buddha and Confucius were pure philosophy, for nowhere is there to be found in their teachings any word signifying a supreme being.

As for the morals of the various systems, they speak for themselves. All except Christianity require good works, and promise salvation on no other terms; while Christianity alone requires nothing but naked faith, a belief in its Savior, and probably a slight sprinkling of cold water.

While there are other appendages attached to it, they are not prerequisites, nor in any way essential to salvation. A man can, under the Christian scheme, remain a hardened criminal all his life, and if he believes at the last moment, he can get from his priest a clean bill of morals on payment of fees, and pass without let or hindrance to the realms of paradise.

It is no wonder that Bauer deemed it the duty of the civil government to suppress this criminal, fraudulent thing, called Christianity. In this opinion all good men should concur, and ask that the millions of dollars expended in support of the church and its mountebanks, be turned over to the poor.

We have made an estimate from the best data we could obtain, from which we find the result to be, that if the money annually wasted in sustaining useless religions were turned into proper channels it would feed and clothe all the poor of the world.

Conflict Between Science and Religion

There is no room to question the fact that science and religion are, as they ever have been, in deadly conflict.

Astronomy has filled endless space with worlds and systems of worlds that have existed from eternity. Religion has created but a single world, our little earth, and lighted it, for the sole benefit of man, with a little sun and moon, and a few little stars, all made in a single day, and created out of nothing.

Science reveals our earth as a globe revolving on its axis and around the sun.

Religion makes the earth a flat surface, and carries the sun around it. Religious man, in his ignorance, stops the sun to fight his battles, while science tolerates no quietude in the universe.

Religion created the first man a perfect being; science found him a savage. Religion put him in a paradise; science found him in a wilderness. Religion degraded him as time passed on, while science advances him in the scale of humanity and reason.

Religion created this earth about 6,000 years ago, and peopled it in the short space of six days; science goes back countless millions of years to find its beginning, and then carries it through other millions of years before man made his appearance on it. Religion finds a powerful being, in the image of a man, residing in the heavens, who out of nothing made the universe! Science finds force or gravitation to be a property of matter, and a sufficient cause for the existence and maintenance of the universe. Science teaches that planets are born, live to old age, and die; that they begin as tenuous gas, become fluid, solidify, live in the vegetable and animal epochs, and finally, like our moon, revolve as dead bodies; that our sun and other suns are still in their infancy, in time to become solid bodies fit for habitation.

What Is Life?

What is life? is a question asked by some of the ablest naturalists; and they further ask, whether it is unchangeable and indissoluble matter permeating the universe and creating the forms of life, or whether it is ordinary matter of aggregated atoms, returning to its original elements when its work is done.

Modern science, says Huxley, sustains the latter hypothesis; under whatever guise it takes refuge, whether fungus or oak, worm or man, the living protoplasm not only dies and is resolved into its mineral constituents, but it is always dying that it may live: protoplasm, in whatever form, is the germ of life; all forms of protoplasm contain carbon, hydrogen, oxygen, and nitrogen; and science has failed, with the microscope or otherwise, to discover the slightest difference between the protoplasm of the animal and that of the plant. Man, beast, fowl, reptile, fish, mollusk, worm, and polyp are composed of clustered units of the same character of protoplasm, with a nucleus; and this is equally true of plants.

Traced back to its earliest state, the plant rises as does man in a particle of nucleated protoplasm, which is the basis of all life. The plant raises the less complex substances of carbonic acid, water, and ammonia to living protoplasm, while the animal can raise only complex substances of dead protoplasm to living protoplasm. Remove from the living protoplasm either carbonic acid, water, or ammonia, and life ceases. The rays of the sun produce the same disturbances on the protoplasm of the plant and animal, creating nucleated action, resulting in growth in both, and vital action in the animal. The vegetable receives support from mineral and atmospheric substances, while the animal must take its nourishment from the vegetable and other animal matter; but life as an abstract quality or quantity is produced by the combined action of light, heat, and water. Every exertion, mental or physical, of the animal results in a loss of vital force, to be renewed only by a draft on the source of vitality. The decomposed rocks are held in solution and acted on by light and heat, which create disturbances in the materials, causing the aggregation of homogeneous molecules to form chemical combinations. A single molecule is first formed into a cell, to which, by the law of affinity, others are added, forming an aggregate of cells, and in the end constituting the lowest form of vegetable life, thereby laying the foundation, from which evolve, first the lower, and finally the higher forms of animal life.

H. C. Bastian, professor of anatomy and physiology in the London University (1880), says: "An attentive consideration of mental phenomena of living beings fails to assure us of the existence of the mind as a self-existent entity. It is quite the reverse. Very many of those who are the most entitled to form a judgment upon this subject regard it as a legitimate inference, from existing knowledge, that conscious states, and, indeed, mental phenomena, are dependent on the properties and molecular activities of nerve tissues, just as magnetic phenomena are dependent on the properties and molecular action of certain kinds or states of iron...Reflex action consists of ingoing fibers continuous in a nerve center with so-called sensory nerve cells, which in their turn are in communication with some group or groups of motor nerve cells, whence issue outgoing fibers for the transmission of stimuli to muscles. Such groups are continually increasing in number and structural development during animal progress. We shall find in reflex action support for the doctrine that the nervous system generally is to be regarded as the organ of mind, and as the nerve system continues to grow, intelligence would be thus subject to actual growth."

In concluding this subject, it may be said, there can be no doubt, so far as our knowledge goes, founded on anatomy, physiology, chemistry, and the other sciences, that mind is the result of the flex and reflex action of the nervous system, set in motion by coming in contact with external objects through one or more of our sensory organs, thereby producing mental and physical phenomena. But all this does not settle the vital question of life, for science is incapable of determining the full scope of the source of mental and physical activity. And, as I understand him, this is just where Professor Huxley leaves the matter.

In his "Evolution of Life," Dr. H. W. Mitchell tells us that life is a form of chemical force acting on organic substances through the law of affinity; that a group of chemical compounds known as albuminoids enter largely into animal bodies, as well as into the most of our food; that this subtle force of chemical affinity possesses the power of so combining and arranging atoms or molecules as to form other and more complex bodies, such as changing gases into jelly-like albuminous compounds called protoplasm, which is the first step in the evolution of vital organisms endowed with the principle called life.

Conclusion

Every system of religion, whatever may have been its status in former times, must in this day of free thought and advanced science be able to stand the test of criticism and reason, or it must take its place among the fables, legends, and myths of the dead past. Many of the ancient systems, resting on, if possible, better foundations than the present living ones, have passed into oblivion, leaving doubtful manuscripts and more enduring monumental inscriptions of their influence and power over the minds and bodies of men. The great and powerful religious systems of Chaldea, Babylon, Egypt, Scandinavia, Persia, Greece, and Rome, which so long swayed the destinies of the world, and were accepted as divine and immortal truths, have passed away to sleep in the grave of eternity; while in India, the cradle of all religions, and in China, these institutions are struggling in their death-throes.

Judaism is a thing of the past, vibrating between life and death, its soul having already departed, leaving the body to be claimed for burial by strangers.

And, last of all, Christianity is on trial, not for its murder of thirty or forty millions of innocent men, women, and children, and other crimes, but for its claim to be of supernatural origin.

Criticism, science, history, reason, and common sense are the prosecuting witnesses, and they have been brought into court as the result of free thought and free speech, in spite of the strenuous efforts of the church to crush them.

Listen to Byron while he says

"Even Gods must yield, religions take their turn,
'Twas Jove's, 'tis Mahomet's; and other creeds will rise
With other years, till man shall learn
Vainly his incense soars, his victim bleeds.
Poor child of doubt and death, whose hope is built on reeds."

Dr. L. Buchner, the great German scientist, in his "Man in the Past, Present, and Future," speaking of Christianity, says: "It stands, by its dogmatic portion or contents, in such striking and irreconcilable, nay absolutely absurd contradiction with all the acquisitions and principles of modern science, that its future tragical fate can only be a question of time."

We are living in an age of reason and common sense, an age of science and toleration, an age of progress and growing humanity. The world is better than it was in the dark ages; man is better to-day than he was yesterday; and he will be better to-morrow than he is to-day. Even the mythologian is betraying signs of awakening humanity. Whether life be the result of force acting on organized forms, and dependent on such forms for its existence, or whether it be independent matter, residing in such organized forms and self-existent, science gives no response. And whether life is to continue beyond the grave is a problem resting on the hidden and immutable laws of nature, the key to which is as accessible to the insect and the quadruped as to the scientist or the priest. Man in his onward course is no longer a slave to superstition.

The mythologian may lament his fading glory, he may hurl his anathemas, he may bewail his declining influence, he may parade his pit of torment, and he may call upon his self-made divinities to hurl their thunderbolts, while the sensible world smiles with contempt at his childish simplicity.

The church has lost its power to use instruments of torture and to apply the torch to an unbelieving world. The loss of this power carries the church down with it; its death is only a question of time.

When the mythologian shall have shuffled off his clerical garb, and when his doctrines, his dogmas, his superstitions, and his nonsense have all to the grave gone down, may the world forgive and forget his errors, his crimes, and his intolerance, while his ashes repose in peace and tranquillity under the ever-watchful care and guidance of Horus, Ra, and Tum, where no bugle's blast shall wake him to battle again.

Printed in the USA
CPSIA information can be obtained
at www.ICGtesting.com
LVHW022206090224
771078LV00004B/648